Directing Successful Projects with PRINCE2™

London: TSO

Published by TSO (The Stationery Office) and available from:

Online
www.tsoshop.co.uk

Mail, Telephone, Fax & E-mail
TSO
PO Box 29, Norwich, NR3 1GN
Telephone orders/General enquiries: 0870 600 5522
Fax orders: 0870 600 5533
E-mail: customer.services@tso.co.uk
Textphone 0870 240 3701

TSO@Blackwell and other Accredited Agents

Customers can also order publications from:
TSO Ireland
16 Arthur Street, Belfast BT1 4GD
Tel 028 9023 8451 Fax 028 9023 5401

First published 2009

ISBN 978 0 11 331060 9

Printed in the United Kingdom for The Stationery Office
N6021139   c30   06/09

Contents

List of figures

List of tables

Foreword

PRINCE2™ is extensively used in more than 150 countries around the world, and its take-up grows daily. It is widely considered as the leading method in project management, with in excess of 20,000 organizations already benefiting from its pioneering and trusted approach.

This new publication is aimed at supporting the senior manager responsible for a project, specifically those managers undertaking an executive role on a project for the first time. Covering the duties and behaviours expected of members of the Project Board, *Directing Successful Projects with PRINCE2* can be used as a reference at any stage to check what is required. It is intended to be used in conjunction with the revised version of *Managing Successful Projects with PRINCE2* (TSO, 2009).

The updated guidance will help those running projects of any size and in any environment to effectively deliver what is required by appropriately managing the costs, timescales, quality, scope, risks and benefits. Its development has followed widespread consultation and draws upon the real-life experiences of organizations in both the public and private sectors.

The number of people taking PRINCE2 qualifications increases by around 20% year on year, and it remains a key contributor to the successful delivery of projects. It is a vital method for any organization wishing to secure efficient and effective operational outcomes.

Nigel Smith

Chief Executive

Office of Government Commerce

Acknowledgements

The Office of Government Commerce (OGC) has continued to develop and improve the definition and presentation of PRINCE2 within this reference manual. The authoring team are acknowledged for their significant contribution, under contract, to the design and development of this guidance.

Lead author

Andy Murray	Outperform UK Ltd

Authoring team

Nigel Bennett	Sun Microsystems Ltd
John Edmonds	pearcemayfield
Bob Patterson	Fujitsu Services
Sue Taylor	APMG PRINCE2 examiner
Graham Williams	GSW Consultancy Ltd

Further contributions

In order to ensure that OGC's *Directing Successful Projects with PRINCE2* (2009) remains a true reflection of current and future trends in the international field of project management best practice, and to produce guidance with lasting value, OGC consulted widely with key stakeholders and experts at every stage in the process. OGC would like to thank the following individuals and their organizations for their contributions to this new guidance:

PRINCE2 reference group

Rob Brace Department of Work & Pensions; Andrew Bragg, Chief Executive, APM; Prof. Christophe Bredillet, ESC Lille; Terry Cooke Davis, Human Systems; Lynne Crawford, University of Sydney; John Cutting, MOD (DPA – DE&S); Prof. Darren Dalcher, Middlesex University, National Centre for Project Management; Steve Falkenkrog, PMI; Ruth Little, DTI Projects Centre; Dusty Miller, Sun Microsystems Ltd; Bob Patterson, Fujitsu; Philip Rushbrook, Cabinet Office; Beverley Webb, BSI Project Management standard committee; Jens Wandel, Director, UNDP

PRINCE2:2009 project governance

Mike Acaster, OGC, Project Executive; Eddie Borup, BPUG; Senior User; Anne-Marie Byrne, TSO, Project Manager; Janine Eves, TSO, Senior Supplier; Sandra Lomax, BPUG, Senior User; Richard Pharro, APMG, Senior Supplier

Reviewers

Robert Allen, PRS for Music; Adalcir da Silva Angelo, Elumini IT & Business Consulting; Paul Askew, Housing Corporation; Richard Aspden, Pathfinder Project Management; Gareth Atwood, Foster Wheeler Energy; Marc Baetens, Pronohau Ltd; Andrew Ball, Audit Commission; Jim Barker, Curtis & Cartwright Consulting Ltd; Keith Batchelor, Foster Wheeler Energy; Dick Bennett, APMG Chief Assessor; Colin Bentley, PRINCE2 Chief Examiner 1998–2008; Johan Bleeker, Standard Bank; Eddie Borup, Ibps solutions; Chris Braithwaite, Wellstream; George Brooke, Oak Lodge Consulting Ltd; Mark Canning, North West Regional Development Agency; Tim Carroll, Standard Chartered Bank; Jacqueline Chadwick, VOSA; Alison Clack, Sean Alison Ltd; Jim Clinch, Clinch Consulting; Brian Coombes, The Projects Group; Arthur Coppens, Getronics Consulting Educational Services; Bjarne Corvinius, Rovsing Management; Anthony Dailey, MWH; Terry Dailey. Deliverables Management Consultants; Hassan El Meligy, IEEE; Darilyn Evans, Adaptive Frameworks; Alan Ferguson, AFA; Chris Ferguson, Novare Consulting Ltd; Ray Frew, Aspen Management Training; Alvin Gardiner, PR-02 (Scotland) Ltd; Emmanuel Gianquitto, APMG (International); Colin Graham, Aylesbury Vale DC; John Greenwood, CSC; Angelika Hamilton, APMG (Germany); Gary R O Haran Doyle, Swiss Life; Simon Harris, Logical Model Ltd; Wietse Heidema, Opmaat Consultancy & Training; Luis Herrera, Consultant; Terry Hewins, Land Registry; Nigel Jones, AJS; Howard Joseph, Home Office; Ravi Joshi, Action For Children; Hans Kemper, APMG (Netherlands); Eddie Kilkelly, ILX Group plc; Lawrie Kirk Tanner, James Management Consultants (Australia); Wieslaw Kosieradzki, P2Ware; Eddie Lamont, Lothian & Borders Police; Tony Levene, Quality Projects; Martin Lewis, Lucid IT; David Lillicrap, London Borough of Ealing; Steve Livingstone, BNFL; Tim Lulham, Network Rail; Maria Maltby, Charnwood Borough Council; Dusty Miller, Sun Microsystems Ltd; Trevor Mirams, Parity; Adrian Newton, Quorum ICT; Bruce Nicholls, Bryan Cave; Helen Nicoll, NHS; Chris Price, Highways Agency; G. Raghunandan,

Satyam Computer Services Ltd; Geoff Rankins, Goal Professional Services Pty Ltd; Lizz Robb, Yellowhouse.net pty Ltd; Graham Robertson, Serco; Eileen Roden, PM Professional Learning; Philip Rushbrook, Cabinet Office; Ian Santry, Home Office; Andrew Schuster, Department of Health; Noel Scott, Symantec; John Sherwood, Highways Agency; Joy Shewring, APMG (USA); Jay M. Siegelaub, Impact Strategies LLC; Raed M. Skaf, Oger Systems Ltd; Tim Sneller, Southend-on-Sea Borough Council; Rod Sowden, Aspire Europe Ltd; Rob Sucher, Armstrong Webb; Mark Sutton, SCOLL Methods Ltd; Ian Thomas, Liberty Network Consultancy; Dot Tudor, TCC; Bram de Vuyst, Getronics Consulting Management Services; Jens Wandel, United Nations Development Programme; Sheryl Ward, Skandia; Peter Weaver, Corte-grande; David Whelbourn, Xwave solutions inc; Stephen Wierzbicki, Bristol Management Centre; Jorn Wigh, APMG (Denmark); Gerald Williams, Projectlabs; Philip Wilson, Cabinet Office

Directing Successful Projects with PRINCE2 pilot group

The British Council; Capital Coast District Health Board; Department of Labour (New Zealand); Fishserve; Metropolitan Police; Ministry of Economic Development (New Zealand); Ministry of Education (New Zealand); Staffordshire Metropolitan Borough Council; Standard Bank; Suffolk County Council; Sun Microsystems Ltd; Vietnamese Academy of Social Sciences.

Conventions used in this manual

Throughout this manual, the following terms use title case:

- PRINCE2 themes
- PRINCE2 processes
- PRINCE2 roles
- Defined management products

Activities within PRINCE2 processes will always be referred to using the same key words or phrases, and are not otherwise distinguished, as they should be evident from their context. For example, 'The Project Board will give ad hoc direction in these circumstances.'

Abbreviations and acronyms have largely been avoided; however, where they are used, they will be spelt out in full on first use.

Key points are illustrated like this:

> A PRINCE2 project has continued business justification.

Example techniques are illustrated like this:

> **Example of a prioritization technique – MoSCoW**
>
> Each acceptance criterion is rated as either **M**ust have, **S**hould have, **C**ould have or **W**on't have for now (MoSCoW).
>
> All the 'Must have' and 'Should have' acceptance criteria should be mutually achievable.

Introduction

1 Introduction

1.1 THE PURPOSE OF THIS MANUAL

PRINCE2 (Projects in a Controlled Environment) is a structured project management method based on experience drawn from thousands of projects – and from the contributions of countless project sponsors, Project Managers, project teams, academics, trainers and consultants. This manual is designed:

- For managers taking on senior project roles, either for the first time or for the first time in a PRINCE2 context
- As a reference guide for managers who are more experienced in directing projects and/or using PRINCE2 but who nevertheless wish to check the detailed guidance on specific topics
- As a source of information on PRINCE2 for senior managers considering adopting the method.

It covers the questions frequently asked by those people who sponsor or direct projects:

- What's expected of me?
- What should I expect of the Project Manager?
- How do I know the Project Manager is applying PRINCE2 appropriately?
- How do I delegate authority to the Project Manager but keep control?
- What decisions am I expected to make?
- What information is required/available to help me make decisions?
- How do we tailor the use of PRINCE2 for projects of differing scale or type?
- What does an effective Project Board look like?

1.2 THE STRUCTURE OF THIS MANUAL

The manual is structured as follows:

- Chapter 1 explains how to use this manual; why projects are different from business-as-usual activities; the importance of a structured approach to managing projects; and the benefits of using PRINCE2
- Chapter 2 provides an overview of PRINCE2 and introduces some key terms and concepts

- Chapter 3 describes the duties and behaviours (what's expected) of the Project Board and expands on the related aspects of PRINCE2
- Chapters 4 to 10 describe the Project Board activities, providing a route through the PRINCE2 project lifecycle from a Project Board perspective
- Chapter 11 outlines factors that should be considered in tailoring PRINCE2 for different types and sizes of project and outlines a systematic tailoring approach
- Appendix A contains Product Description outlines which provide guidance on the purpose, composition, format and quality criteria of some of PRINCE2's management products
- Appendix B deals with project governance
- Appendix C outlines the responsibilities for each PRINCE2 role
- The glossary contains a list and explanation of the terms used in this manual
- Further information provides useful reading references that can supplement the knowledge and point practitioners towards further research sources.

1.3 HOW TO USE THIS MANUAL

It is important to emphasize that PRINCE2 is not a rule book prescribing a one-size-fits-all approach to projects but a flexible method that can readily be tailored to the context of a specific project.

It is not expected that this manual will be read from start to finish. Chapters 4 to 10 are designed as 'point in time' reference guides that Project Board members can dip into for guidance which is pertinent to the activity that the Project Board is expected to perform. Each of these chapters contains:

- The purpose of the activity
- What to expect from the Project Manager
- The actions required of the Project Board
- Area of focus for each Project Board role (Senior User, Senior Supplier, Executive, Project Assurance)

- Suggested Project Board agendas
- A checklist for the activity.

The appendices provide additional reference material to help Project Board members review and approve management products (Appendix A); to understand the totality of the responsibilities for each role in the project management team (Appendix C); and to understand the specific use of project management terms used in a PRINCE2 project (Glossary).

Those people unfamiliar with PRINCE2 should read the rest of Chapter 1 and Chapters 2, 3 and 11 fully.

Project Managers, Team Managers, Project Assurance and Project Support personnel should read *Managing Successful Projects with PRINCE2* (2009) which describes the method specifically for their roles.

1.4 THE IMPORTANCE OF PROJECT MANAGEMENT

Senior managers are accountable for two aspects of an organization's performance:

- Maintaining current business operations – profitability, service quality, customer relationships, brand loyalty, productivity, market confidence etc. What we term 'business as usual'
- Improving business operations in order to survive and compete in the future – looking forward and deciding how business change can be introduced to best effect for the organization.

As the pace of change (technology, business, social, regulatory etc.) accelerates, and the penalties of failing to adapt to change become more evident, the focus of management attention is inevitably moving to achieve a balance between business as usual and business change.

Projects are the means by which we introduce change – and, while many of the skills required are the same, there are some crucial differences between directing business functions and directing project work.

1.5 WHAT MAKES PROJECTS DIFFERENT?

There are a number of characteristics of project work that distinguish it from business as usual:

- **Change** Projects are the means by which we introduce change
- **Temporary** As the definition in section 2.1.1 states, projects are temporary in nature. Once the desired change has been implemented, business as usual resumes (in its new form) and the need for the project is removed. Projects should have a defined start and a defined end
- **Cross-functional** Projects involve a team of people with different skills working together (on a temporary basis) to introduce a change that will impact others outside the team. Projects often cross the normal functional divisions within an organization and sometimes span entirely different organizations. This frequently causes stresses and strains both within organizations and between, for example, customers and suppliers. Each has a different perspective and motivation for getting involved in the change
- **Unique** Every project is unique. An organization may undertake many similar projects, and establish a familiar, proven pattern of project activity, but each one will be unique in some way: a different team, a different customer, a different location. All these factors combine to make every project unique
- **Uncertainty** Clearly, the characteristics already listed will introduce threats and opportunities over and above those we typically encounter in the course of business as usual. Projects are more risky.

Given that (1) projects are the means by which we introduce business change, and that (2) project work entails a higher degree of risk than other business activity, it follows that implementing a secure, well-proven project management method is a valuable business investment.

1.6 THE PRINCE2 APPROACH TO PROJECT MANAGEMENT

PRINCE2 is a non-proprietary method and has emerged worldwide as one of the most widely accepted methods for managing projects. This is largely due to the fact that PRINCE2 is truly generic: it can be applied to any project regardless of project scale, type, organization, geography or culture.

PRINCE2 achieves this by isolating the management aspects of project work from the specialist contributions, such as design, construction etc. The 'specialist activities' would clearly be different in, say, a hospital construction project from those for an aircraft procurement project. The specialist aspects of any type of project can be easily plugged into the PRINCE2 method. This means that industry-specific models – variously known as 'engineering models' or 'project lifecycles' – can be used, alongside PRINCE2, to provide the most secure framework possible for project work.

Moreover, any specialist project lifecycle defined in terms of its products can very easily be integrated in a PRINCE2 framework as the method facilitates the integration of the management and specialist activities through its focus on products. PRINCE2 defines all the management products that will be required (Business Case, plans, roles, reports, registers etc.) to manage the project adequately and provides a reliable product-based planning technique that creates a set of Product Descriptions for the project's deliverables. Each Product Description defines the purposes, composition, derivation (source inputs), quality criteria and quality methods that will apply to the product concerned – so that there is an unambiguous, common understanding of the work involved.

Because PRINCE2 is generic and based on powerful structural concepts, organizations adopting the method as a standard can substantially improve their organizational capability and maturity across multiple areas of business activity, such as business change, construction, IT, mergers and acquisitions, research, product development and so on.

1.7 BENEFITS OF PRINCE2

Before introducing the structure of the method, it is worthwhile reviewing the key benefits of adopting PRINCE2:

- PRINCE2 embodies established and proven best practice and governance for project management
- It can be applied to any type of project – and can easily be implemented alongside specialist, industry-specific models ('engineering models' or 'development lifecycles')
- PRINCE2 is widely recognized and understood, therefore it provides a common vocabulary for all project participants – promoting effective communication

- PRINCE2 provides for the explicit recognition of project responsibilities – so that participants understand each other's roles and needs. There is a defined structure for accountability, delegation, authority and communication
- Its product focus clarifies (for all parties) what a project will deliver, why, when, by whom and for whom
- PRINCE2 plans are carefully designed to meet the needs of the different levels in the project management team, improving communication and control
- It is based on a 'management by exception' framework, providing for the efficient and economic use of management time (whether at corporate, programme, Project Board or project management levels)
- PRINCE2 ensures that participants focus on the viability of the project in relation to its Business Case objectives – rather than simply seeing the completion of the project as an end in itself
- It defines a thorough but economical structure of reports
- It ensures that stakeholders (including sponsors and resource providers) are properly represented in planning and decision making
- Adopting PRINCE2 promotes learning and continual improvement in organizations
- PRINCE2 promotes consistency of project work and the ability to reuse project assets; it also facilitates staff mobility and reduces the impact of personnel changes/handovers
- PRINCE2 is an invaluable diagnostic tool, facilitating the assurance and assessment of project work, troubleshooting and audits
- There are scores of accredited training and consultancy organizations (ATOs and ACOs) operating worldwide, who can supply expert support for PRINCE2 projects or for organizations planning to adopt PRINCE2.

1.8 RELATED OGC GUIDANCE

PRINCE2 is part of a suite of guidance developed by the UK Office of Government Commerce (OGC), which is aimed at helping organizations and individuals manage their projects, programmes and services consistently and effectively. Figure 1.1 outlines the structure of the set.

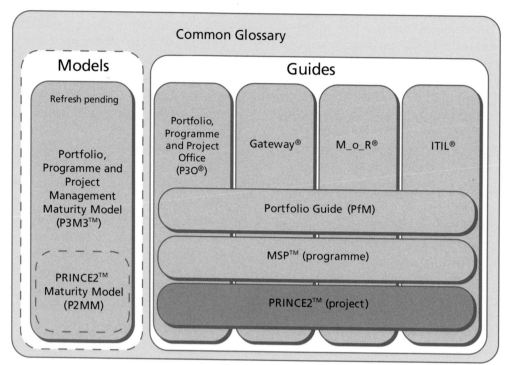

Figure 1.1 OGC best-practice guidance

Where appropriate, OGC methods and guidance are augmented by qualification schemes, and all aspects are supported by accredited training and consultancy services. Details of these best-practice guides and other relevant guides can be found in Further Information.

Overview of PRINCE2 2

2 Overview of PRINCE2

2.1 KEY DEFINITIONS

The following definitions are used in PRINCE2 and are important for understanding the context of the method.

2.1.1 A project

> A **project** is a temporary organization that is created for the purpose of delivering one or more business products according to an agreed Business Case.

PRINCE2 should only be used for managing projects. The 'temporary organization' needs to be big enough or complex enough to justify producing a Business Case and setting up project management controls. If the work can be managed simply as a 'line management' task, using PRINCE2 could create an inappropriate management overhead.

2.1.2 A programme

> A **programme** is a temporary flexible organization structure created to coordinate, direct and oversee the implementation of a set of related projects and activities in order to deliver outcomes and benefits relating to an organization's strategic objectives. A programme may have a life that spans several years.

Clearly, there are similarities between projects and programmes – both are temporary and seek to achieve benefits for the sponsoring organization. But there are also important differences. The key distinction is that a project typically produces or changes something (its products) and is then disbanded. Although the purpose of a project is to deliver changes that will ultimately realize Business Case benefits, it rarely exists long enough to ensure that they are fully delivered. For the most part, the benefits of the undertaking are likely to be accrued after the project is completed.

Moreover, many projects are 'enablers', i.e. their products will not deliver business benefits directly but must be augmented by other activity to produce these benefits. For example, the construction of a hospital building is not sufficient, in itself: the medical, nursing and administrative services, equipment and systems must be in place before the healthcare benefits can be achieved.

Programmes are typically established to coordinate the work of a set of related projects, to manage the outcomes and to realize the aggregate benefits. They are often (but not always) established when organizations decide to transform their operations or services from their 'current state' to an improved 'target end-state'. The functions at the programme level tend to be less focused on delivering specialist products but rather on coordinating the efforts of the various projects so that the resulting transformation is effectively integrated.

OGC has produced a valuable guide for managing programmes of this type, *Managing Successful Programmes* (MSP™), which is fully compatible with PRINCE2.

2.1.3 Project management and PRINCE2

> **Project management** is the planning, delegating, monitoring and control of all aspects of the project, and the motivation of those involved, to achieve the project objectives within the expected performance targets for time, cost, quality, scope, benefits and risks.

The objective of project management is to achieve effective control over the project work. It is logically impossible to exert control over anything without some form of plan. The manager then monitors progress – by comparing it with the plan – and exerts control by taking corrective action where necessary.

By definition, a manager must delegate at least some of the work to others, and there are two distinct aspects to delegation. Firstly, delegation requires leadership skills – notably motivation. Leadership and motivation are not competencies that can be codified in a method, so, although PRINCE2 does help managers to lead effectively (by defining the things they should be doing), it does not directly address interpersonal skills, such as motivating and negotiating. However, there are many other forms of management development and training that can be implemented alongside PRINCE2 to enhance leadership skills.

The second aspect of delegation is that it requires the existence of a hierarchical organization structure within which to delegate. One of the characteristics of project work discussed in Chapter 1 was that it is cross-functional. This means that the line hierarchies we are familiar with in most organizations tend to be ineffective when it comes to managing projects. It is this aspect of delegation that PRINCE2 addresses directly by defining a flexible, temporary organization model with roles and responsibilities that are optimized for project work.

Note also that our definition of project management identifies six performance targets for a project:

- Time
- Cost
- Quality
- Scope
- Risk
- Benefits.

Of course the approach to each of these will have a bearing on the others: for instance, if scope is expanded, time and cost (and possibly risk) will be impacted. Much of project management is about balancing and prioritizing these factors in order to match the needs of corporate or programme management.

The PRINCE2 method provides a comprehensive, flexible and fully integrated set of best practices for setting up an appropriate project management team, establishing plans, monitoring the six performance targets and maintaining control through effective decision making.

One of the strengths of the PRINCE2 structure is the way in which the organization, plans and controls are integrated. Individual good practices can be implemented for many aspects of project management but, to achieve maximum benefit, the various disciplines must knit together in a consistent, workable overall framework – as in PRINCE2.

2.2 STRUCTURE OF PRINCE2

The PRINCE2 method addresses project management with four integrated elements of principles, themes, processes and the project environment (Figure 2.1):

- The principles are essential and must be followed for PRINCE2 to be truly implemented
- The themes address key aspects of project management that must be addressed throughout a project – they apply continually and in parallel

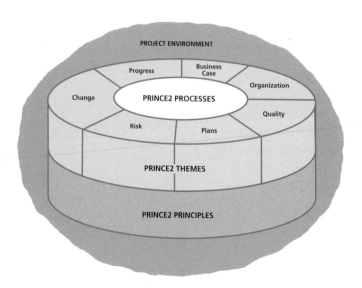

Figure 2.1 The structure of PRINCE2

- The processes describe a step-wise summary progression through the project lifecycle – outlining the detailed activities for directing and managing the project successfully (with references to explanatory guidance in the themes)
- The fourth element is the project environment. This recognizes that PRINCE2 must be tailored to the context of the particular organization and project concerned, taking into account factors such as project size, complexity, type, geography, culture etc.

2.2.1 Principles

The seven PRINCE2 principles are the guiding obligations for good practice that a project should follow if it is using PRINCE2. These are derived from lessons, both good and bad, that have affected project success. If a project does not follow these principles, then it is not using PRINCE2.

The PRINCE2 principles
- A PRINCE2 project has continued business justification
- PRINCE2 project teams learn from previous experience (lessons are sought, recorded and acted upon throughout the life of the project)
- A PRINCE2 project has defined and agreed roles and responsibilities with an organization structure that engages the business, user and supplier stakeholder interests
- A PRINCE2 project is planned, monitored and controlled on a stage-by-stage basis (management by stages)
- A PRINCE2 project has defined tolerances for each project objective to establish limits of delegated authority (management by exception)
- A PRINCE2 project focuses on the definition and delivery of products, in particular their scope and quality requirements
- PRINCE2 is tailored to suit the project's environment, size, complexity, importance, capability and risk.

2.2.2 Themes

The PRINCE2 themes are those aspects of project management that:

- Need to be addressed continually. They are not one-off activities. For example, Risk Management should be central to every decision: it is not a case of updating a register from time to time
- Require specific treatment for the PRINCE2 processes to be integrated effectively. For example, the processes require a division of responsibilities between those people who direct (the Project Board), those who manage (the Project Manager) and those who deliver (the project team) as defined in the Organization theme.

The themes provide guidance on how the process activities should be performed (and explain why). For example, numerous processes in PRINCE2 involve creating or approving plans: explanatory guidance can be found in the Plans theme.

There are seven PRINCE2 themes, as outlined in Table 2.1.

In summary, the set of PRINCE2 themes describe:

- How baselines are established (in the Business Case and Plans themes). The baselines cover all six project performance targets – benefits, risks, scope, quality, cost and time – and act as key reference points for subsequent monitoring and control
- How the project management team monitors and controls the work as the project progresses (in the Progress, Quality, Change and Risk themes).

The Organization theme underpins the other themes with a secure structure of roles, clarifying accountability and offering clear paths for delegation and escalation.

2.2.3 Processes

PRINCE2 provides a process model for managing a project. The processes can easily be scaled and tailored to suit the requirements of all types of project. They consist of a set of activities that are required to direct, manage and deliver a project.

Table 2.1 The PRINCE2 themes

Theme	Description	Answers
Business Case	The project starts with an idea which is considered to have potential value for the organization concerned. This theme addresses how the idea is developed into a viable investment proposition for the organization and how project management maintains the focus on the organization's objectives throughout the project.	Why?
Organization	The organization sponsoring the project needs to allocate the work to managers who will be responsible for it and steer it through to completion. Projects are cross-functional so the normal line function structures are not suitable. This theme describes the roles and responsibilities in the temporary PRINCE2 project management team required to manage the project effectively.	Who?
Quality	The initial idea will only be understood as a broad outline. This theme explains how the outline is developed so that all participants understand the quality attributes of the products to be delivered – and then how project management will ensure that these requirements are subsequently delivered.	What?
Plans	PRINCE2 projects proceed on the basis of a series of approved plans. This theme complements the Quality theme by describing the steps required to develop plans and the PRINCE2 techniques that should be applied. In PRINCE2 the plans are matched to the needs of the personnel at the various levels of the organization. They are the focus for communication and control throughout the project.	How? How Much? When?
Risk	Projects typically entail more risk than stable operational activity. This theme addresses how project management manages the uncertainties in plans and in the wider project environment.	What if?
Change	This theme describes how project management assesses and acts upon issues which have a potential impact on any of the baseline aspects of the project (its plans and completed products). Issues may be unanticipated general problems, requests for change or instances of quality failure.	What's the impact?
Progress	This theme addresses the ongoing viability of the plans. The theme explains the decision-making process for approving plans, the monitoring of actual performance and the escalation process if events do not go according to plan. Ultimately, the Progress theme determines whether and how the project should proceed.	Where are we now? Where are we going? Should we carry on?

The PRINCE2 process model addresses project activity at four levels of management:

- **Corporate or programme management** While not part of the project management team, this higher management level is an important influence as it sets the business context for projects
- **The Project Board** This is the most senior level within the project management team. The Project Board represents three key interests: those of the sponsoring business, the users and the suppliers. The Project Board is accountable for the success of the project within the boundaries set by corporate or programme management. This manual is designed to act as a reference manual for Project Board members

- **The Project Manager** Acts as the single focus for the day-to-day management of the project. The Project Manager has authority to run the project within constraints approved by the Project Board
- **The Team Manager** At the lowest management level in a PRINCE2 project, the Team Manager's prime responsibility is to supervise the creation of the products allocated to the team by the Project Manager. Note that in simple projects the Project Manager and Team Manager roles are often performed by the same person.

The processes are illustrated in Figure 2.2 and summarized below.

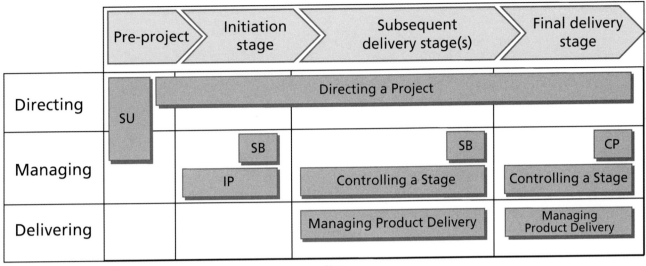

Key
SU = Starting up a Project
IP = Initiating a Project
SB = Managing a Stage Boundary
CP = Closing a Project

Note
- Starting up a Project is used by both the directing and managing levels.
- There should be at least two management stages, the first of which is the initiation stage.
- Managing a Stage Boundary is first used at the end of the initiation stage and repeated at the end of each subsequent stage except the final stage. It is also used to prepare Exception Plans, which can be done at any time including in the final stage.
- For complex or lengthy initiations, Controlling a Stage and Managing Product Delivery can optionally be used to manage the initiation stage.

Figure 2.2 The PRINCE2 processes

Starting up a Project*: this process covers the pre-project activities required to commission the project and to get commitment from corporate or programme management to invest in project initiation by answering the question 'Do we have a viable and worthwhile project?' Project Board members are appointed at this time and detailed guidance is provided in Chapter 4.

Directing a Project: this process describes the Project Board's activities in exercising overall project control. The activities focus on the decision making necessary for Project Board members to fulfil their accountabilities successfully while delegating the day-to-day management of the project to the Project Manager. The activities in the Directing a Project process are described in detail in the following chapters:

- Chapter 5: Authorize initiation
- Chapter 6: Authorize the project

*Note: these processes are explained in this manual to the extent that they impact the Project Board's decision-making activities. They are covered in detail in the companion guide, *Managing Successful Projects with PRINCE2* (TSO, 2009).

- Chapter 7: Authorize a Stage or Exception Plan
- Chapter 8: Give ad hoc direction
- Chapter 9: Authorize project closure

Initiating a Project*: this process describes the activities the Project Manager must lead in order to establish the project on a sound foundation. Every PRINCE2 project has an initiation stage. The key deliverable from this stage is the Project Initiation Documentation which includes an overall Project Plan and defines baselines for the six project performance targets of time, cost, quality, scope, risk and benefits. The Project Initiation Documentation represents an authoritative statement of what the project will deliver, how this will be achieved, and by whom.

Managing a Stage Boundary*: PRINCE2 projects are managed in stages. This process describes the activities the Project Manager must undertake to provide the Project Board with sufficient information to enable it to review the success of the current stage, approve the next Stage Plan, review the updated Project Plan and confirm continued business justification and acceptability of the risks. Therefore, the process should be executed at, or close to, the end of each management stage.

Controlling a Stage*: this process describes how the Project Manager manages the project execution/delivery activity during a stage and reports progress and exceptions to the Project Board.

Managing Product Delivery*: this process addresses the Team Manager's role in supervising the detailed work of creating the specialist products and provides the link between the Project Manager and the teams undertaking the project work.

Closing a Project*: this process describes the closure activity towards the end of the final stage of the project. The Project Manager leads the process which provides for an orderly de-commissioning, including any remaining project acceptance and handover requirements.

2.2.4 The project environment

PRINCE2 can be used on projects irrespective of project scale, complexity, geography, culture etc. PRINCE2 can also be used whether the project is part of a programme or is being managed as a stand-alone initiative. This reflects the principle that PRINCE2 must be tailored to suit the particular project context.

Tailoring refers to the measures taken to apply the method properly to an individual project, ensuring that the amount of governance, planning and control is appropriate – neither too burdensome for a simple project nor too informal for a large or complex project. Further guidance is provided in Chapter 11. The adoption of PRINCE2 across an organization is known as embedding. Table 2.2 sets out the differences between tailoring and embedding.

2.3 THE ROLE OF SENIOR MANAGEMENT IN PRINCE2

This manual is for Project Board members, who represent the most senior level of management in a PRINCE2 project. Project Board members are accountable for the work they direct, but the extent of their business responsibilities is usually much wider than the project. They can rarely afford to get involved in the detail of every project for which they are responsible. This means that the effectiveness with which project work can be delegated is crucial.

The PRINCE2 Organization theme and the carefully integrated planning and control themes solve this problem by setting up an unambiguous framework of responsibilities.

In PRINCE2, the Project Board delegates the management of the project to the Project Manager in a series of stages – each based on an approved Stage Plan. Provided the Project Manager can deliver the stage within the tolerances defined in the plan, there is no necessity for the Project Board members to maintain close contact with the work. The stage boundaries represent major control milestones – when the Project Board reviews whether the Project Manager has delivered the previous stage properly and approves a plan for the succeeding stage. The PRINCE2 processes provide other checks and balances but, essentially, this is how senior managers on the Project Board are able to 'manage by exception'.

Senior managers acting as Project Board members must also provide leadership and direction to ensure that their projects remain aligned to the

Table 2.2 Embedding and tailoring

Embedding (done by the organization to adopt PRINCE2)	Tailoring (done by the project management team to adapt the method to the context of a specific project)
Focus on:	Focus on:
■ Process responsibilities	■ Adapting the themes (through the strategies and controls)
■ Scaling rules/guidance (e.g. score card)	■ Incorporating specific terms/language
■ Standards (templates, definitions)	■ Revising the Product Descriptions for the management products
■ Training and development	■ Revising the role descriptions for the PRINCE2 project roles
■ Integration with business processes	■ Adjusting the processes to match the above.
■ Tools	
■ Process assurance.	
Guidance in PRINCE2 Maturity Model (P2MM)	Guidance in Chapter 11 and in *Managing Successful Projects with PRINCE2* (TSO, 2009)

organization's strategic aims. The Project Board is a guiding coalition that is necessary to support and direct the project. As with company boards, if the composition of the Project Board is deficient then the project is likely to struggle. If the Project Board is affected by in-fighting, the project is almost certainly doomed. Appointing the right Project Board is probably the single most important factor in achieving a successful project.

The PRINCE2 project management team structure is illustrated in Figure 2.3.

In order to be flexible and meet the needs of different environments and different project sizes, PRINCE2 does not define management jobs to be allocated to people on a one-to-one basis. PRINCE2 defines roles, each of which is defined by an associated set of responsibilities. These roles might be allocated, shared or combined according to the project's needs.

The Project Board roles are more fully defined in Appendix C.

2.3.1 The three Project Board roles

2.3.1.1 Executive

Although the Project Board is responsible for the project, the Executive (supported by the Senior User(s) and Senior Supplier(s)) is ultimately accountable for the project's success and is the key decision maker. The Project Board is not a democracy controlled by votes.

The Executive's role is to ensure that the project is focused throughout its life on achieving its objectives and delivering a product that will achieve the forecast benefits. The Executive has to ensure that the project gives value for money, ensuring a cost-conscious approach to the project, balancing the demands of business, user and supplier.

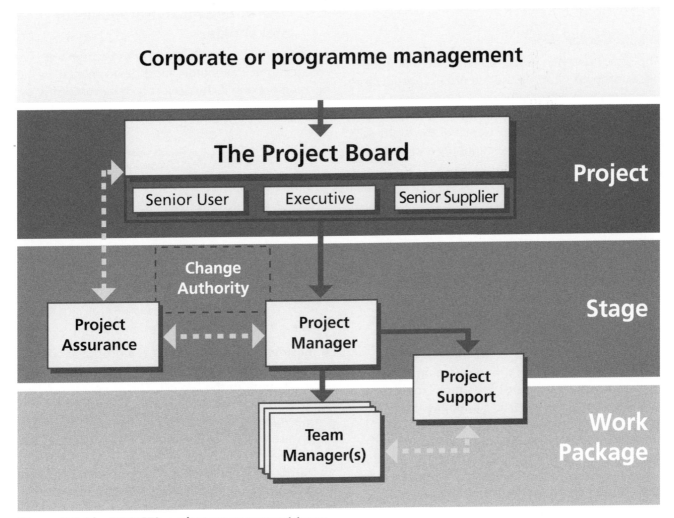

Figure 2.3 The PRINCE2 project management team

The Executive is appointed by corporate or programme management during the pre-project process Starting up a Project. The role of the Executive is vested in one individual, so that there is a single point of accountability for the project. The Executive will then be responsible for designing and appointing the rest of the project management team, including the other members of the Project Board. If the project is part of a programme, corporate or programme management may appoint some or all Project Board members.

Throughout the project, the Executive is responsible for the Business Case.

The Executive needs to be able to exercise a balanced view on behalf of the wider organization. The Senior User(s) must be able to make decisions on behalf of those groups who will use or gain benefit from the project's products. The Senior Supplier(s) must be able to make decisions on behalf of the organization providing the expertise or resources to produce the products.

2.3.1.2 Senior User

The Senior User(s) is responsible for specifying the needs of those who will use the project's products, for user liaison with the project management team and for monitoring that the solution will meet those needs within the constraints of the Business Case in terms of quality, functionality and ease of use.

The role represents the interests of all those who will use the project's products, those for whom the products will achieve an objective or those who will use the products to deliver benefits. The Senior User role commits user resources and monitors products against requirements. This role may require more than one person to cover all the user interests. For the sake of effectiveness, the role should not be split between too many people.

The Senior User also represents the interests of those who will maintain the specialist products of the project after closure. Exceptions to this do occur, such as when an external supplier maintains the products in service/operation as part of a maintenance/support agreement. In fact, the distinction is not really important. What matters is that operations, service and support interests are represented appropriately from the outset.

As the beneficiary of the benefits, the Senior User(s) is held to account and must demonstrate to corporate or programme management that the forecast benefits that were the basis of project approval are, in fact, realized. This is likely to involve a commitment beyond the end of the life of the project.

2.3.1.3 Senior Supplier

The Senior Supplier represents the interests of those designing, developing, facilitating, procuring and implementing the project's products.

This role is accountable for the quality of products delivered by the supplier(s) and is responsible for the technical integrity of the project. This role will include providing supplier resources to the project and ensuring that proposals for designing and developing the products are feasible and realistic.

If necessary, more than one person may be required to represent the suppliers.

2.3.2 The three primary categories of stakeholder

It is a PRINCE2 principle that the three primary categories of stakeholder must be involved in decision making if the project is to be successful, as shown in Figure 2.4.

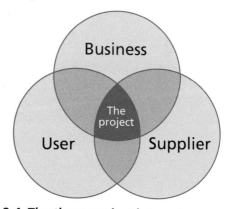

Figure 2.4 The three project interests

- **Business** The products of the project should meet a business need that will justify the investment in the project. The project should also provide value for money. The business viewpoint, therefore, should be represented to ensure that these two prerequisites exist before a project commences and remain in existence throughout the project. The Executive role is defined to look after the business interests.

■ **User** PRINCE2 makes a distinction between the business interests and the requirements of those who will use the project's outputs. The user viewpoint should represent those individuals or groups for whom some or all of the following will apply:

- They will use the outputs of the project to realize the benefits after the project is complete
- They will operate, maintain or support the project's outputs
- The outputs of the project will impact them.

The user presence is needed to specify the desired outputs and ensure that the project delivers them. The Senior User(s) will represent this stakeholder interest on the Project Board.

■ **Supplier** The creation of the project's outputs will need resources with certain skills. The supplier viewpoint should represent those who will provide the necessary skills and produce the project's products. The project may need to use both in-house and external supplier teams to construct the project's products. The Senior Supplier(s) will represent this stakeholder interest on the Project Board.

Logically, if the result of the project fails to meet the requirements of any of these three interests, the project has been unsuccessful. PRINCE2 dictates that in order to ensure that the three interests are satisfied, they must be represented effectively in the project management team.

The three interests are safeguarded by ensuring that they are represented on the Project Board and in the **Project Assurance** roles. It is the Project Board's responsibility to assure itself that the project is being conducted correctly. The Project Board members each have a specific area of focus for Project Assurance: namely business assurance for the Executive, user assurance for the Senior User(s) and supplier assurance for the Senior Supplier(s). Project Board members may delegate assurance responsibilities to other qualified personnel (if they do not have time to undertake the assurance activities or do not have the specialist knowledge required). Assurance personnel must be independent of the Project Manager but the intention is that the roles should be supportive. The Project Manager is responsible for the day-to-day running of the project; the assurance roles are there to provide advice and support, not direction.

The level of overlap between the interests of the business, user and supplier will change according to the type of corporate organization and project: for example, if a project uses an in-house supplier, the business and user interests will be more likely to overlap than if an external supplier is used.

Note: the term **customer** is also used in PRINCE2, normally in the context of a commercial customer/supplier relationship. 'Customer' can usually be interpreted as a collective term for the business and user interests. However, one example of an exception to this broad rule would be where an organization is developing a new product to bring to market. In this case the business interest is aligned with that of the supplier and 'customer' equates simply with 'user'. Where the user interest is external to the organization sponsoring the development, as in this example, it still needs to be represented in some way – perhaps by the sales/marketing function.

As well as the primary categories of stakeholder interests (business, user and supplier), which should be represented on the Project Board, there will be a wider range of stakeholders who may affect, or be affected by, the project. These stakeholders may be internal or external to the corporate organization and may either support, oppose or be indifferent to the project. Effective engagement with these stakeholders is key to a project's success.

2.3.3 The Senior Responsible Owner role

The Senior Responsible Owner (SRO) role has been introduced widely in the UK Government sector for large projects and programmes and is now used increasingly by others. The standard definition for the role is below.

> The **Senior Responsible Owner** is the single individual with overall responsibility for ensuring that a project or programme meets its objectives and delivers the projected benefits.

It should be stressed that the SRO is not a PRINCE2 role. However:

■ In the programme context, the Executive would report to the SRO appointed at programme level. It might also be appropriate for the SRO to act as the Executive for major projects within the programme

■ Where an SRO is appointed in the context of a single large project, the person undertaking the SRO role would also undertake the Executive role or appoint the person who will undertake the Executive role.

2.4 WHAT PRINCE2 DOES NOT PROVIDE

PRINCE2 is not designed to cover every aspect of project management.

As already explained, PRINCE2 does not directly address interpersonal skills, such as leadership and motivation. Though highly important, these aspects cannot be codified in a process or method.

Some methods, tools and techniques are specific to project type, context or the host corporate environment. PRINCE2 excludes these aspects because they are not generic – but the structure of PRINCE2 and its product focus simplifies and facilitates the integration of specialist models, methods and techniques.

Lastly, there are some generic aspects of project management which have been excluded because they are already covered by a range of well-established methods and techniques. Examples in this category are organizational change management, techniques for estimation and scheduling (such as Delphi or critical path analysis), budgetary control techniques (such as earned value analysis), purchasing and contract management. Again, these aspects can very easily be integrated within an overall PRINCE2 framework.

Project Board duties
and behaviours

3

3 Project Board duties and behaviours

The **duties of the Project Board** are to:

- Be accountable for the project
- Provide unified direction
- Delegate effectively
- Facilitate cross-functional integration
- Commit resources
- Ensure effective decision making
- Support the Project Manager
- Ensure effective communication.

To understand fully the Project Board's responsibilities in the project's lifecycle, it is important to be aware of the underlying duties and the behaviours they imply.

Why is this important? The fact is that surveys frequently cite **lack of executive/senior management support** as one of the top causes of project failure.

3.1 BE ACCOUNTABLE FOR THE PROJECT

The **Project Board** is accountable for the success (or failure) of the project.

The Project Board is accountable, to programme or corporate management, for the success or failure of the project within the constraints defined in a project mandate.

Being accountable means accepting and demonstrating 'ownership' of the project. The project Executive is seen as the focus of accountability for the project, and accordingly retains the ultimate decision-making authority. However, projects require the interests of all three stakeholder categories (business, user and supplier) to be satisfied in order to be successful. This means that there is an obligation on Senior User(s) and Senior Supplier(s) to ensure that the interests of their respective areas are safeguarded.

For instance, Senior User(s) are accountable for ensuring that the products of the project will enable the intended benefits to be realized operationally. If this does not happen, the project may be considered 'successfully' completed for some, but the business benefits may never be realized.

Senior Supplier(s) are accountable for ensuring that the products of the project are reliable, properly integrated, can be maintained efficiently etc. If this does not happen, the later stages of the project are likely to be fraught with problems, with repeated failures – or benefits might be offset by operational maintenance difficulties after project closure.

Consequently, it is part of the project Executive's responsibility to ensure that the other Project Board members are selected carefully and perform their roles effectively.

Also, given that the project Executive has the ultimate decision-making authority, it is important that the Executive has the requisite level of authority in practice. If other Project Board members are more senior in the corporate or programme management organization, it may prove difficult for the Executive to manage their contributions effectively. This situation can arise on a programme if the Programme Manager also acts as the Executive on some projects but is out-ranked in the line organization by other Project Board members.

Project Board members are busy managers and they may feel insecure about being accountable for project work with which they may have relatively little contact. In PRINCE2, Project Board members exercise this accountability by ensuring that personnel with the right skills and experience are involved in the team and in Project Assurance roles. The disciplines PRINCE2 uses to promote effective delegation and management by exception (see section 3.3) also serve to build Project Board members' confidence and encourage them to accept accountability.

3.2 PROVIDE UNIFIED DIRECTION

Project Board members must provide unified direction.

Unified direction is about teamwork at Project Board level. While each Project Board member has accountability for satisfying the interests of a particular stakeholder category, it is crucial that a cohesive overall direction for the project is agreed and communicated.

Clearly, this can involve difficult compromises. As far as possible, Project Board members need to defer to each other's areas of accountability and work to achieve mutually agreed solutions. Frequently, the best solution to a problem cannot be determined by objective evaluation: it is simply the one that Project Board members can agree on. Users may favour a project approach or solution that suppliers consider inappropriate – perhaps because it is incompatible with an established strategy/standard, or is expensive to support. Project Board members need to resolve such issues (focusing on the likely impact on business benefits) and communicate the outcome in a way that minimizes any potential for friction.

> **Example of lack of unified direction**
>
> In an internal IT project for an international company based in New York, the Senior Supplier was perceived as having more influence in the company than the non-IT project Executive. The Senior Supplier was a long-serving senior manager with a lot of experience and a network of contacts, whereas the project Executive was a relatively young member of the team, recently appointed as manager of the overall programme.
>
> The Executive and the Senior Supplier differed over aspects of the international IT strategy agreed for the overall programme. The Senior Supplier had sufficient business influence to be able to resist its implementation on the project concerned, which was at the core of the programme. The disagreement at Project Board level caused uncertainty and delays in the project work. Irrespective of the rights and wrongs in the debate about strategy, the problem was that decision making was disrupted and decisions were evaded because of internal politics, which the project Executive was not sufficiently senior to resolve.
>
> Eventually, corporate management became impatient with the lack of momentum and the result was that the entire Project Board and the senior programme management team were replaced.

In the boxed example, lack of unified direction was clearly a factor in delaying the project – exacerbated, in that case, by the Executive not having sufficient authority to make a final decision.

What is clear is that where unified direction breaks down, and Project Board members communicate perceptibly different agendas, the effect is very rapidly translated into reduced overall project momentum and/or conflicting activity at the project team level. Unified direction applies whether the customer/supplier relationship is internal to the organization or a commercial relationship.

3.3 DELEGATE EFFECTIVELY

> Project Board members must delegate effectively, using the PRINCE2 organizational structure and controls designed for this purpose.

Several aspects of PRINCE2 are designed to promote effective delegation, e.g.:

- The well-proven framework of roles and responsibilities in the project management team
- Plans designed to meet the needs of managers at different levels.

A key feature of the method in this respect is the implementation of management stages – delegating the day-to-day management of the project to the Project Manager on a stage-by-stage basis.

PRINCE2 projects are divided into a succession of management stages (time-slices which do not overlap) and this provides benefits both in terms of planning and progress control.

3.3.1 The 'stage contract'

The best way to understand how PRINCE2 expects the Project Board to delegate the management of stage activity to a Project Manager is to view the Stage Plan as a 'notional contract'. The terms of this notional contract are outlined in the box below.

> **The stage contract**
>
> The Project Board undertakes, collectively, to:
>
> - Provide overall direction
> - Commit the resources in the plan.
>
> The Project Manager undertakes, subject to approved tolerances, to:
>
> - Deliver the stage products
> - Meet the product quality criteria
> - Deliver within the stage budget
> - Meet the target completion date.

Delegating in this manner entails a degree of trust between Project Board members and the Project Manager, but PRINCE2 also provides checks and balances:

■ The Project Board will normally require the Project Manager to produce Highlight Reports at intervals throughout the stage to confirm that the stage remains on track
■ The Project Board members may employ Project Assurance measures to confirm that their various stakeholder interests are being safeguarded at the working level (e.g. part-time assurance roles or periodic independent health checks).

With these arrangements, the PRINCE2 project proceeds to completion as a series of stage contracts, minimizing the formal participation required of the Project Board.

However, this pattern can only work if there is also an understanding of how the Project Manager must behave if things do not go to plan, i.e. if an exception arises – covered in section 3.3.2.

The same contract analogy can be applied to the Project Plan.

Table 3.1   The six tolerance areas by level

Tolerance areas	Project level tolerances	Stage level tolerances	Work Package level tolerances	Product level tolerances
Time +/- amounts of time on target completion dates	Project Plan	Stage Plan	Work Package	NA
Cost +/- amounts of planned budget	Project Plan	Stage Plan	Work Package	NA
Scope Permitted variation of the scope of a project solution, e.g. MoSCoW prioritization of requirements (Must have, Should have, Could have, Won't have for now).	Project Plan (note 1)	Stage Plan (note 1)	Work Package (note 1)	NA
Risk Limit on the aggregated value of threats (e.g. expected monetary value to remain less than 10% of the plan's budget); and Limit on any individual threat (e.g. any threat to operational service)	Risk Management Strategy	Stage Plan (note 2)	Work Package (note 2)	NA
Quality Defining quality targets in terms of ranges, e.g. a product that weighs 300g +/- 10g	Project Product Description	NA (note 3)	NA (note 3)	Product Description
Benefits Defining target benefits in terms of ranges, e.g. to achieve minimum cost savings of 5% per branch, with an average of 7% across all branches	Business Case	NA	NA	NA

Note 1 – the scope of a plan is defined by the set of products to be delivered. Scope tolerance (if used) should be in the form of a note on or reference to the product breakdown structure for the plan. Scope tolerance at the stage or Work Package level is of particular use if applying a time-bound iterative development method such as Agile.

Note 2 – more specific stage level risk tolerances may be set by the Project Board when authorizing a stage or by the Project Manager when commissioning Work Packages, especially from external suppliers.

Note 3 – quality tolerances are not summarily defined at the stage or Work Package level but are defined per Product Description within the scope of the plan.

3.3.2 Exceptions and escalation

The way PRINCE2 handles 'exceptions' (i.e. departures from approved plans) depends on the implementation of tolerances. Tolerances are the permissible deviation above and below a plan's target for time and cost without escalating the deviation to the next level of management. There may also be tolerance levels for quality, scope, benefit and risk. Tolerances are applied at project and stage level and may also be implemented at the level of individual Work Packages.

If tolerances are not implemented ('zero tolerance'), Project Managers have no clear measure of discretion if things do not go to plan – and however they react, there is likely to be criticism:

■ If every minor exception is escalated to the Project Board, the Project Manager is merely monitoring the work and making no effort to implement corrective action – clearly unsatisfactory from the Project Board members' point of view. In effect, the Project Board is having to do the Project Manager's job
■ On the other hand, if the Project Manager carries on working to put things right, implementing corrective actions, there is the risk that Project Board members will see this as exceeding the Manager's (unwritten) discretion – and question why the problems were not escalated earlier: the Project Manager is seen as taking on the Project Board's role in this instance.

Table 3.1 describes where tolerances may be usefully applied and shows in which management product they are documented.

Employing tolerances at stage level is essential to the way the Project Board delegates and empowers the Project Manager, and to the exception management process. Stage tolerances provide a defined area of discretion within which the Project Manager can be left to manage. The rule is that if the Project Manager forecasts that the stage cannot be completed within the agreed tolerances, an exception must be escalated to the Project Board.

The Project Board should be informed (or Project Assurance should be consulted) of any circumstances where tolerances could potentially be exceeded but forecasts suggest that the stage can be recovered.

Tolerances for budget and schedule are illustrated in Figure 3.1. In this example, the budget tolerance is £160k to £220k and the time tolerance is +/- 2 weeks. (Note: the plus and minus values do not have to be the same.) As long as the stage is forecast to be completed within these tolerance targets, the Project Manager does not need to seek additional approvals from the Project Board.

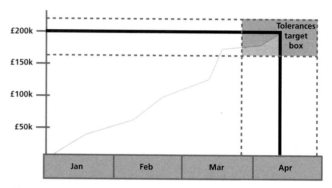

Figure 3.1 Stage tolerances for budget and schedule

When an exception does occur, the Project Manager escalates, initially, in the form of an **Exception Report**. The Exception Report serves to alert Project Board members to the situation and outline any different responses that are available – recommending a way forward if possible. Once the way forward has been agreed, the Project Manager may be asked to produce an Exception Plan. Using the contract analogy again, escalation is necessary because the current stage contract is no longer viable and must be replaced as soon as possible by a new 'contract' in the form of an Exception Plan.

Setting aside the problems that may have caused the situation to arise, raising an exception is evidence of good project management and Project Board members should, wherever possible, respond positively.

It is not unusual for the Project Board members to be the first to recognize an exception, e.g. when changes arise in the wider programme or business environment that will have a significant impact on the project in question. In this context, it is the responsibility of the Project Board to alert the Project Manager – but the exception planning approach is otherwise the same.

Should the exception relate to project level tolerances, the Project Board will need to escalate to corporate or programme management as it means that the project is forecast to go beyond the authority given to the Project Board.

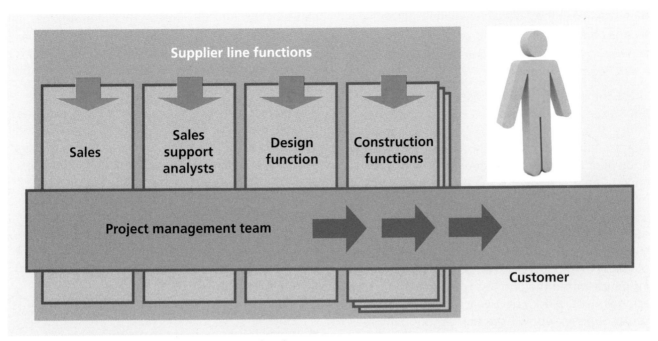

Figure 3.2 Cross-functional project organization

3.4 FACILITATE CROSS-FUNCTIONAL INTEGRATION

The **project management team** is a temporary, almost always cross-functional, structure set up with specific responsibility for the project. Project Board members must ensure that this is recognized and respected in the functional or line management organization(s), and that the Project Board's authority is not undermined.

The organizational structures within which projects are undertaken can vary on a continuum between the strictly functional type at the one extreme and the 'projectized' at the other. Most fall somewhere in between the two extremes and employ various styles of 'matrix management'.

Projects are typically cross-functional. That is, they cross internal line function boundaries in organizations or involve entirely separate business entities. If this characteristic does not apply, i.e. the business, user and supplier interests all come from the same organization and the same line function, the work involved is not really a project – it can be managed more simply as a line 'task'.

Figure 3.2 illustrates a relatively common supplier project. None of the line functions in this supplier organization see the whole picture – they each contribute differently to the solution for the customer. For the project to succeed, a customer-facing matrix organization needs to be set up to integrate the efforts of the various contributing line functions and engage with the customer – this is the PRINCE2 project management team.

In effect, the supplier's line functions are supplying services to the project in the form of specialist quality capabilities, people and/or products.

Services supplied to a project may take two forms:

- **Resources:** e.g. the design function supplies a designer to the project. This arrangement is sometimes termed a 'strong project matrix' because the work is directly managed by the project
- **Products:** e.g. the design function supplies the completed design. This is termed a 'weak project matrix' because the line function manages the work on behalf of the project.

The two types of matrix each have advantages and disadvantages – and projects frequently consist of a mixture of the two. Strong matrixes, with dedicated resources, tend to be able to respond faster when changes or problems occur but can be wasteful of resources. Weak matrixes are often implemented to optimize resourcing but at the expense of flexibility and project response.

Difficulties arise when the engagement between the project and the line functions is ineffective. For example:

- **A resource** is not available when required
- **A product** is not delivered on time
- Products from different line functions do not 'fit together' properly.

These common types of problem may be caused by poor project planning (e.g. providing inadequate notice of requirements) or by conflicting line management priorities, by shortages of resources or by poor communication between the project and/or line functions. It is the Project Manager's job to try to establish plans and agreements that anticipate and, where possible, eliminate these obstacles. Ultimately, though, Project Board members carry much more authority than Project Managers – and it is crucial that they use this influence within the business to ensure that matrix arrangements work effectively for the project (the Senior Supplier would have this responsibility in the example in Figure 3.2).

If the roles of project and line management relative to one another are not clear and efficient, there will be continual stress in the delivery process – with inevitable consequences on performance. The extent to which problems like this can be avoided usually depends on the extent to which PRINCE2, or the 'project culture', is embedded in the overall organization. Some organizations are much more project-oriented than others. This means that the temporary project management teams are recognized and accorded a degree of authority similar to (or even higher than) the permanent line functions within the business. The PRINCE2 Maturity Model (P2MM) provides valuable additional guidance on embedding a project culture and improving overall project performance within organizations.

3.5 COMMIT RESOURCES

Project Board members are responsible for committing the resources necessary for the successful completion of the project.

In selecting Project Board members, it is an important criterion that, collectively, they should be able to deliver all the resources required for the success of the project.

Project Board members may be motivated to trim resources in order to cut costs. This is not unreasonable, but planning decisions should be carefully thought through, examining relevant assumptions, experience and lessons learned. The costs and penalties caused by under-resourcing a project can often be out of proportion to the initial (perceived) savings.

The Project Manager is responsible for assembling the plans, and for identifying, communicating and agreeing the resource requirements with suppliers. The Project Board must approve the plan for the work to commence. It is important that Project Board members understand that, by approving a Project Plan or Stage Plan, they are endorsing it as a realistic plan and undertaking to commit the resources required. Project Board members cannot subsequently distance themselves and blame the planners.

Nevertheless, many factors can disrupt the process:

- It may not be possible to agree a resource plan that allows the project to meet other constraints, e.g. on budget or schedule
- Resources that have been agreed may, in the event, become unavailable
- Project delays or other changes may alter the timing of resource requirements with the result that they cannot be met
- Where personnel are committed part-time, project work may be interrupted by competing business-as-usual activity or contributions on other, higher-priority projects.

Many of these problems, particularly with internal resource providers, arise from competing business or line management priorities, and Project Board members must decide where the project fits in relation to the competing priorities. By the same token, Project Board members will also carry more weight in negotiations and disputes with external suppliers.

Resourcing issues are typically the ones most frequently escalated to Project Board members, and resourcing generally provides the best opportunities for Project Board members to demonstrate senior management commitment and support for the Project Manager.

Where Project Board members fail to provide adequate support, resources may get deployed on the basis of whoever shouts loudest, resulting in unnecessary antagonism and at the expense of rational decision making.

3.6 ENSURE EFFECTIVE DECISION MAKING

Project Board members must ensure effective decision making.

It is the Project Board that makes the key decisions in the project. Decision making is the means by which control is exerted, and PRINCE2 provides an optimized framework for this purpose.

3.6.1 Progress control

Second only to setting direction, the Project Board is primarily a progress control function. Progress is authorized by means of approving the Project Plan and Stage Plans. Approval should be given collectively by Project Board members to ensure that all stakeholder interests are understood and safeguarded.

Plans are approved and progress is assessed and reaffirmed at Project Board reviews, the main ones being at stage boundaries. Clearly, it is preferable for Project Board members to meet – physically if at all possible but, failing that, using video or telephone conferences.

Project Board reviews are all based on essentially the same simple agenda, as shown in the boxed example. It can be seen that the reviews should always focus on plans, approving them and assessing progress in relation to them.

Example of a typical Project Board agenda

1 Look back

Review status in relation to the current Stage Plan (or Exception Plan)

2 Look forward

Preview the next Stage (or Exception) Plan

3 Assess overall project viability

Consider the current status of the Business Case, Project Plan and issues/risks

4 Make a decision

Decide whether to give authorization to proceed by approving the next Stage Plan (or Exception Plan)

The agenda is organized this way so that Project Board members are fully briefed on the current context of the project work before stepping back from the detail (in agenda item 3) to assess the position in relation to the overall Project Plan and, most importantly, the Business Case.

3.6.2 Risks, issues, changes and exceptions

Decisions on minor risks, issues and changes can usually be delegated to the Project Manager. On complex projects, or if there is a high volume of change at the working level, the Project Board may alternatively delegate day-to-day decisions in this area to a Change Authority specially established for the purpose. However, some decisions must be reserved for the Project Board. Who makes decisions on what category of risks, issues and changes should be agreed when initiating the project and documented in the Project Initiation Documentation.

There is an opportunity for this at Project Board reviews (agenda item 3). However, decisions about risks, issues and changes are frequently made in the course of the Directing a Project process activity of giving ad hoc direction (see Chapter 8) as and when required during the stages.

When issues result in an exception, the Project Board should, again, express its decision in terms of approving a plan; in this case an Exception Plan. The generic agenda outlined in the boxed example remains valid for Project Board reviews prompted by exceptions.

This agenda and the pattern of Project Board decision making are further expanded in the discussion of detailed Project Board activities in Chapters 4 to 10.

3.6.3 Quality control

The Project Board contributes to quality control by approving:

- The overall Project Product Description (including customer quality expectations and acceptance criteria)
- The Quality Management Strategy (including key quality responsibilities)
- The individual Product Descriptions for key project deliverables.

PRINCE2 provides a useful technique to confirm whether a product fulfils its requirements through **quality reviews**. Project Board members may or may not be the best-qualified people to participate in such reviews. What matters is that Project Board members ensure that the right people are involved in quality reviews and other quality-related responsibilities.

Senior Users need to know that people with the right practical experience are being involved at the working level and in quality inspections/reviews. Similarly, Senior Suppliers need to know that the right specialist technical expertise is being brought to bear. The focus of the Executive's concern is the quality of adherence to good project management practice and standards, including PRINCE2.

This is not to say that Project Board personnel cannot act as quality reviewers, rather that they should do so only where they bring relevant skills, knowledge or experience – and not simply in their capacity as Project Board members. Consequently, they are more likely to be involved in reviewing the project's management products, such as plans, than the specialist technical products.

In whatever context, PRINCE2 aims to bring the right people together and provide them with the right information so that they can make the right decisions.

At the Project Board reviews held at stage boundaries, the Project Manager will use information in the Quality Register to reassure Project Board members that the agreed quality measures have been implemented and the right people have been involved.

3.6.4 Project Assurance

Delegating to Project Assurance personnel who are responsible for monitoring the business, user and supplier interests at working level is another means by which Project Board members can ensure that decisions are well-informed. Project Assurance can be implemented in a variety of different forms, e.g. with part-time or full-time personnel or with occasional, independent project health checks.

Irrespective of the form it takes, a delegated Project Assurance function carries no accountability for the project. It is important that the Project Board's accountability (for the project) and the Project Manager's responsibilities (for the stages) are not undermined.

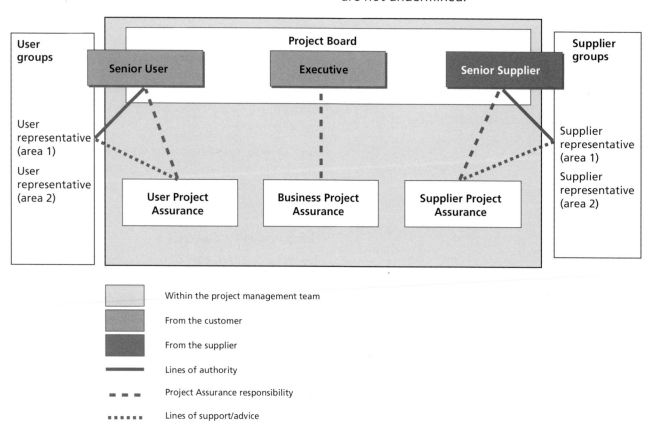

Figure 3.3   Use of advisory boards

Project Assurance is simply another opportunity to make the right people and the right information available for decision making.

3.6.5 Informal contributions to decision making

Another consistent feature of PRINCE2 is that the formal reviews (Project Board end stage assessments and quality reviews) are regarded as incentives for the Project Manager and the team to get things agreed informally beforehand.

At Project Board reviews, particularly, there should be no surprises. There is rarely enough time at a Project Board review to examine the plans in detail but Project Board members will nevertheless want to be confident about what they are signing up to. It follows that the Project Manager will wish to discuss and resolve as many of the important or contentious aspects of plans beforehand – and it is important that Project Board members provide effective channels for this to happen. These may be channels for direct contact or, if Project Board members really are too busy, reliable arrangements for Project Assurance personnel to act as intermediaries.

3.6.6 Advisory boards

In larger, more complex projects, there may be several discrete user stakeholders and/or supplier interests – too many to accommodate in a manageable Project Board. A device often used in these circumstances is to introduce user and/or supplier advisory boards, chaired respectively by the Senior User or the Senior Supplier (see Figure 3.3).

As with a delegated Project Assurance role, advisory boards do not carry any accountability for the project, but they provide valuable support and guidance for Project Board members by helping to define the approaches preferred by that stakeholder group.

If advisory boards are used, it can be useful to delegate user assurance to the user advisory board and supplier assurance to the supplier advisory board.

3.7 SUPPORT THE PROJECT MANAGER

> Project Board members must provide effective support for the Project Manager.

The Project Manager is the focus for the day-to-day management of the project work and this is often a busy and stressful role. The Project Board can relieve some of this stress and remove some of the obstacles by demonstrating visible and sustained support for the Project Manager.

There are many means of achieving this:

- Ensure that the Project Manager is sufficiently experienced and properly equipped for the scale of the project involved
- Emphasize to all concerned that the Project Manager carries the Project Board's delegated authority during stages – and reinforce this if it is challenged
- Provide unified and consistent direction
- Commit resources for the approved plans
- Use influence to ensure that, wherever possible, the resources committed in plans are actually delivered
- Provide for adequate Project Support (see section 4.5.8), so that the Project Manager can communicate and lead without getting bogged down in formalities and administrative work
- Listen carefully to the Project Manager's advice and consider what should be done to remove any obstacles. Act as a mentor, where appropriate
- Allow time for planning – exerting pressure to 'get started' on the deliverables is a common failing
- Implement supportive Project Assurance arrangements
- Be readily accessible for consultations, advice and guidance
- Respond promptly and constructively when issues are escalated
- Participate in all the formal Project Board reviews.

There is always the possibility that the Project Manager does not measure up to the role. This may become evident in the contacts with the Project Board or come to light as a result of Project Assurance concerns. In these circumstances, the Project Board should discuss the problems in private and determine, if necessary, how to engage a replacement with minimum disruption to project progress or morale. Organizations are generally sensitive to how effectively this type of situation is managed – personnel and stakeholders will respond well if a handover is conducted calmly and professionally. If there is prevarication or open dispute, confidence in the overall project management will be undermined.

Where an important change is necessary in the project management team (not just the Project Manager) – for whatever reason – a PRINCE2 stage boundary provides a logical and convenient opportunity for the handovers.

3.8   ENSURE EFFECTIVE COMMUNICATION

> The Project Board must ensure that communication is timely and effective, both within the project and with the key external stakeholders.

The Project Board is responsible for directing project communication with stakeholders – as champions for the project. On large or complex projects there may be a wide range of stakeholders, including the public. In this type of project a formal Communication Management Strategy will be essential. On simple projects the communications channels and messages may be agreed more informally.

Important aspects to consider are:

- Who are the audiences (internal and external) for project communication?
- How will they be impacted by the project? Sometimes there may be negative impacts and communications must be particularly sensitive
- What are the most appropriate channels in each case – personal contacts, reports, email, newsletters, websites, press releases etc?
- What are the key messages? These should:
  - Be mutually consistent
  - Be consistent with the Project Plan/Stage Plans
  - Be timely: issuing a lot of messages to stakeholders early in a project can result in a perceived lack of momentum later on. It is preferable to time communications to coincide with demonstrable progress. On the other hand, as the handover to operational

implementation approaches, stakeholders who have not been directly involved with the project may be anxious about its impact and are likely to need more information and reassurance
  - Set realistic expectations – in particular, qualify estimated budgets and target completion dates carefully according to the level of confidence in them; quote ranges rather than absolute values until there is confidence in the detail
- When to communicate? A common problem is too much communication from different projects at the same time. Corporate and/or programme communication functions should be able to assist with this – employing a wider communication management strategy.

The essential internal project communication is covered by PRINCE2 project controls – plans, Work Package definitions, Highlight Reports, End Stage Reports etc. Supplementary and 'social' communications such as newsletters are often useful but they should not obscure the basic information flows.

Highlight Reports and **End Stage Reports** can also be used to keep line managers outside the immediate project management team informed. This is sensible in that it avoids duplicating reports, but it can occasionally lead to unnecessary interventions by stakeholders outside the project management team – and this, in turn, can cause unnecessary friction. It is important to communicate and reinforce the accountability of Project Board members (for directing project activity) and Project Managers (for managing it) in the wider organizational culture, so that managers outside the project management team know the correct channels for communicating with the project.

Communication is considered vital in many aspects of modern life but 'getting it right' in projects, as in other spheres, involves achieving a balance. Busy people appreciate information that is 'just in time', i.e. enough to meet their needs at that point in time. Offer too much communication and the audiences may become jaded, switch off and then miss important messages. Give too little and people may become anxious or suspicious about what the project is doing.

Project Board members are responsible, in particular, for communicating effectively with the programme or corporate management sponsoring the project. Perceptions at that level are crucial to continuing business visibility and support. In order to ensure that consistent and accurate messages are communicated, Project Board members often 'reserve' the exclusive right to communicate at this level.

In devising a Communication Management Strategy for the project, careful attention must also be given to any non-disclosure agreements (NDAs) or other considerations of commercial confidentiality or security.

Starting up a Project

4 Starting up a Project

Purpose

The purpose of the Starting up a Project process is to ensure that the prerequisites for initiating a project are in place by answering the question 'Do we have a viable and worthwhile project?'

Nothing should be done until base information (needed to make rational decisions about the commissioning of the project) has been defined, key roles and responsibilities have been resourced and allocated, and a foundation for detailed planning is available.

The purpose of the Starting up a Project process is as much about preventing poorly conceived projects from being initiated as it is about approving the initiation of viable projects. As such, the Starting up a Project process is a lighter task compared to the more detailed and thorough Initiating a Project process. The aim is to do the minimum necessary in order to decide whether it is worthwhile to even initiate the project.

What to expect from the Project Manager

The Project Manager should provide assistance and advice to the Executive and other Project Board members during the development of an outline Business Case, and should take the lead in assembling a Project Brief and a Stage Plan for initiation.

4.1 CONTEXT

The aim of the Starting up a Project process (see Figure 4.1) is to assemble enough information (in a Project Brief) to plan the effort required to initiate the project (in an Initiation Stage Plan) and to evaluate whether it is worthwhile initiating (in an outline Business Case). These activities are regarded as pre-project.

The Starting up a Project process is triggered by corporate and/or programme management issuing a project mandate.

PRINCE2 prescribes that:

- The reasons for undertaking the project are understood – see section 4.2
- Someone is appointed to be accountable for the success of the project and to provide ongoing direction (the Executive) – see section 4.3
- Someone is appointed to be responsible for the day-to-day management of the project (the Project Manager) – see section 4.3
- Lessons from previous similar projects are incorporated – see section 4.4
- The rest of the project management team is designed and appointed – see section 4.5
- The outline Business Case is prepared – see section 4.6
- The project's purpose is clarified and agreed in sufficient detail to enable the project to be initiated – see section 4.7

Starting up a Project process

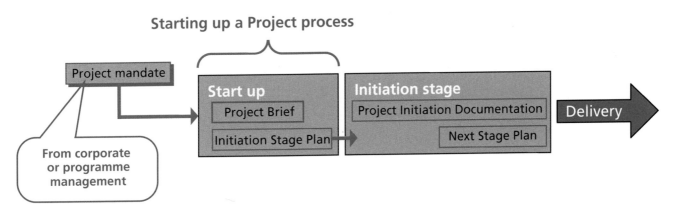

Figure 4.1 Starting up a Project

■ The activities to initiate the project are planned and approved before any significant expense is incurred – see section 4.8.

Where the project is part of a programme, the Starting up a Project process can usually be streamlined. The outline Business Case and the Project Brief may be created at the programme level and the programme will usually appoint some, if not all, members of the Project Board.

4.2 CONFIRM THE UNDERSTANDING OF THE PROJECT MANDATE

PRINCE2 calls whatever information is provided by corporate or programme management to trigger the project the project mandate. Examples may include:

■ A feasibility study
■ A recommendation from a previous project
■ A recommendation from an audit
■ A directive from a regulator
■ A programme plan
■ A business plan
■ An action from a management meeting
■ A request for a proposal (in a commercial environment)
■ Even a phone call or email from the Chief Executive!

As the project mandate can come in many forms, it can also come with varying degrees of completeness. A 'just do it' directive from a management meeting is likely to generate a lot of questions before the expectations and scope of the project are sufficiently well understood for the project to be initiated. On the other hand, a feasibility study is likely to contain all the information necessary to proceed quickly to the initiation activities.

'Emergent projects' can arise from concurrent, uncoordinated activities within an organization. In this case the project mandate may simply be a directive to coordinate a set of existing initiatives in order to secure a more coherent outcome.

The project mandate as a minimum should define the responsible authority for the project and provide sufficient information to be able to identify suitable candidates for the Executive role in order to proceed with the Starting up a Project process.

4.3 APPOINT THE EXECUTIVE AND THE PROJECT MANAGER

To get anything done in a project, you need a decision maker (the Executive) and someone to undertake the planning (the Project Manager).

4.3.1 Select the right Executive

The primary role of the Executive is to look after the interests of the business. The project should meet a worthwhile business need and give value for money. Therefore, the Executive is the person ultimately accountable for the project's success.

See Appendix C for the responsibilities of the Executive.

It is important to ensure the Executive has the following four key characteristics:

■ **Authority**   As the Executive is accountable for the project, the person chosen must have sufficient authority and seniority to make strategic decisions about project direction
■ **Credibility**   The Executive's credibility within the organization will affect his or her ability to lead and direct the project
■ **Ability to delegate**   A key part of the Executive's role is to ensure that the Project Manager is empowered and 'given enough space' to manage the project, i.e. by ensuring that Project Board members operate at the right level. Project Board members should not be involved in the detail of how the project is managed or in the specialist content of the project
■ **Availability**   An Executive who meets all the above characteristics is of little value to the project if he or she is not available to make decisions, provide direction and support the Project Manager.

Consider aligning the Executive's performance objectives with the success of the project.

The Executive should have at least an equivalent level of authority to that of any of the other Project Board members. Authority is not always the same as rank – it can be influenced considerably by factors such as 'office politics' which are rarely explicit.

4.3.2 Select the right Project Manager

One of the most important decisions a newly appointed Executive will make is who to appoint to manage the project.

The choice of Project Manager will be based on aspects of the project, such as its importance to the business, its urgency, size, duration, technical complexity, political complexity, type (construction, IT, product development etc.) and, perhaps, the clarity of the requirements. These must be matched against the capabilities, experience and availability of candidates.

The Executive should also consider whether the quality of the working relationship with the Project Manager is likely to be effective. For example, for a business-critical project, it is advisable for the Project Manager to have worked with the Executive previously and for there to be an established relationship of trust. For a simple project, there may be an opportunity for the Executive to work with a relatively junior Project Manager for the first time.

Project Managers' own preferences might also be a factor. Some Project Managers prefer longer, more stable projects; others prefer shorter more volatile projects. The primary requirement for a Project Manager is that they must have good project management skills. Project Managers should not be appointed for their domain expertise alone (e.g. technical knowledge).

The availability of the right candidate should be given careful consideration. If a suitable candidate is not available, could one be made available? How would the impact of transferring a candidate from another project compare with the impact of not having the right Project Manager on this project? Should a Project Manager be contracted from an external supplier? What impact would this have on internal candidates?

Even if there is a mismatch between the ideal candidate and the person actually appointed, PRINCE2 provides the Project Board with a robust framework for delegation, which facilitates control.

4.4 CAPTURE PREVIOUS LESSONS

There may be a number of significant and relevant lessons derived from earlier projects of a similar type – whether within organizations involved in the project or from other organizations. It is much better to learn by other people's mistakes or successes. Lessons about weaknesses or strengths of the processes, methods, techniques and tools used previously should be reviewed, wherever possible, to see if there is anything of value that could be used on the project.

At this point, it may be a cursory, high-level consideration of lessons, making the way for a more detailed review by the Project Manager during the initiation stage.

Example of learning from lessons from external sources

A city council wanted to reduce the costs of administering taxi cab licences while making it easier for taxi drivers to apply for or renew their licences on-line.

The Project Manager found useful lessons from two sources outside the organization. Another city council explained that its take-up of similar on-line applications was very low because most taxi cab drivers were from disadvantaged areas and did not have internet access or the inclination to use it. However, a charity provided valuable advice on encouraging disadvantaged users to get engaged and use the internet. This guidance was successfully incorporated into the project.

4.5 DESIGN AND APPOINT THE PROJECT MANAGEMENT TEAM

Having identified an Executive and the Project Manager, the next activity is to design the wider project management team. Factors for consideration are the project's size and complexity and the areas that will be impacted by the project outcomes. It is then crucial to design a project management team with appropriate business, user and supplier representation and with a suitable level of Project Support resource.

The aim of the PRINCE2 project management team structure is to get the right people in place (i.e. with the right authority, experience and knowledge), making the right decisions in a timely manner. See Chapter 2 for an explanation of the PRINCE2 project management team structure.

Note that the PRINCE2 project management team structure is defined in terms of roles which do not equate to full-time individuals. That is, one person may have more than one role, a role may be part-time, or a role may be shared by more than one person. However, there are some common-sense rules that must be observed:

- There must only be one Executive and one Project Manager
- Project Board members may perform Project Assurance but they do not undertake other project roles
- Project Assurance roles must always be independent of the Project Manager, Team Manager(s) and Project Support.

4.5.1 The Project Board

One of the PRINCE2 principles is that roles and responsibilities in the project must safeguard the interests of the three stakeholder categories. The Executive, Senior User and Senior Supplier roles make up the Project Board and represent these vital – business, user and supplier – interests, as described in Chapter 2 and the role descriptions in Appendix C.

The Project Board has authority and responsibility for the project within terms of reference set by corporate or programme management (initially contained in the project mandate). The remit includes:

- Defining what is required from the project
- Authorizing the funds for the project
- Committing the resources
- Communicating with external stakeholders.

Project Board members must have the requisite authority. They are the decision makers, responsible for committing resources to the project, such as personnel, finance and equipment. Factors such as the budget, scope and importance of the project will determine the seniority of the Project Board members in the participating organizations.

Frequently, Project Board members will be from senior management positions and their Project Board responsibilities will be in addition to their normal line responsibilities. The concept of 'management by exception' provides for them to be kept regularly informed of progress by the Project Manager so that their contribution is focused on decision making at key points in the project.

Project Board members should ideally be assigned to stay with the project throughout its life, though changes may be inevitable sometimes. A typical example would be where a major external supplier has to be selected part way through a project. In this case, the procurement function of the business may provide a Senior Supplier initially who may be joined, later, by a representative from the selected supplier. Where changes have to be made, minimal disruption occurs when this is undertaken at the end of a management stage.

For a major or high-profile project, being appointed to a Project Board on the expectation that this will be for the whole duration of the project may be seen as limiting career progression. If the right people are to be encouraged to work on business-critical projects, organizations need to arrange incentives appropriately so that success is properly rewarded.

4.5.2 The Executive

The Executive has already been appointed at this point – see section 4.3.1.

4.5.3 Senior User

The Senior User represents the interests of the users of the project's products, and/or those most affected by its outcome.

The Senior User is responsible for monitoring that the project will meet the users' needs by:

- Providing user resources to the project
- Defining acceptance criteria for the project
- Ensuring the project's products are specified in line with the users' needs
- Maintaining business performance stability during transition from the project to 'business as usual'
- Ensuring that the benefits of the project are realized (post-project this will be in the capacity of a functional manager rather than the Senior User as the role does not exist post-project).

See Appendix C for the Senior User's responsibilities.

4.5.4 Senior Supplier

The Senior Supplier represents the interests of those designing, developing, procuring and/or implementing the project's products. The Senior Supplier is responsible for developing products that will meet the requirements of the Senior User, within the cost and time parameters for which the Executive is accountable. This role will include providing supplier resources to the project and ensuring that proposals for designing and developing the products are feasible and realistic.

The Senior Supplier also represents the interests of those who will maintain the specialist products of the project after closure, e.g. engineering maintenance and support. Exceptions to this do occur, e.g. when an external supplier is delivering products to a customer who will maintain them in service/operation: in this instance the operations and maintenance interests are more likely to be represented by a Senior User. In fact, the distinction is not really important – what matters is that operations, service and support interests are represented appropriately from the outset.

4.5.5 The Project Manager

Normally, the Project Manager will have been appointed at this point – see section 4.3.2.

4.5.6 Team Manager(s)

Team Managers' responsibilities are to ensure that the products allocated to them by the Project Manager are created in line with agreed Product Descriptions. Team Managers report to, and take direction from, the Project Manager.

In the permanent line structures of the participating organization, there is often also a reporting relationship between one or more Team Managers and the Senior Supplier. It is vital that any such links are understood and project roles are documented so that conflicts are avoided and the Project Manager's authority is not undermined.

In appropriate circumstances – and often for simple projects – the roles of Project Manager and Team Manager may be assigned to the same person.

4.5.7 Project Assurance

Project Board members are responsible for the aspects of Project Assurance aligned to their respective areas of concern – business, user or supplier. They may conduct their own Project Assurance activities or appoint other, independent, managers or specialists to undertake specific Project Assurance roles. For example, a corporate or programme-level quality manager may be appointed to take on a Project Assurance role.

Project Assurance is not just an independent check, however. Personnel involved in Project Assurance are also responsible for supporting the Project Manager, by giving advice and guidance on issues such as the use of corporate standards or the correct personnel to be involved in different aspects of the project, e.g. quality inspections or reviews.

Where Project Assurance tasks are shared between Project Board members and other individuals, it is important to clarify each person's responsibilities. Anyone appointed to a Project Assurance role reports to the Project Board member for the interest concerned – and must be independent of the Project Manager.

Examples of Project Assurance tasks include, but are not limited to:

- Reviewing the outline Business Case (particularly for business assurance)
- Checking that the project approach is technically correct and in line with corporate or programme strategy (supplier assurance)
- Confirming that the Quality Management Strategy includes the required standards (all assurance interests)
- Ensuring all risks are identified, with suitable ownership and responses (all assurance interests)
- Checking the Product Descriptions are unambiguous (all assurance interests)
- Advising Project Board members on issues of detail (all assurance interests)
- Advising the Project Manager on suitable people to select as quality reviewers or change impact assessors (all assurance interests).
- Acting as independent, or peer, reviewers in product quality reviews (all assurance interests).

Where projects are part of a programme, the programme office (or Programme Management Office, PMO) will often supply Project Assurance resources. However, if implemented inappropriately, this arrangement can undermine the accountability of Project Boards and Project Managers. It must be clear that programme offices do not carry any accountability for the project, and that any authority must be exercised through the Project Board or the Project Manager.

Example of Project Assurance

The gateway reviews recommended by the UK Office of Government Commerce (OGC) are examples of the types of assurance reviews that can be conducted at programme or project level.

These involve a team of experienced people, entirely independent of the project management team, who conduct reviews at key decision points throughout the project or programme. Though not conducted by the internal Project Assurance personnel, these are, nevertheless, a type of Project Assurance measure that may be available to the Project Board.

4.5.8 Project Support

All projects will require some amount of administrative work. Project Managers need to be free to lead and communicate and, if the administrative burden compromises their ability to do so, they should be able to delegate this type of activity to a Project Support resource.

Project Support can involve general administrative services or specialist support for the processes, methods and tools in use on the project, e.g. for configuration management. Many organizations set up project offices to provide systematic support for a number of projects.

Where programmes of related projects are established, programme offices have additional scope and benefits – but, again, care must be taken not to undermine the authority of the Project Board and Project Manager.

Project Support and Project Assurance roles are separated in order to preserve the independence of Project Assurance.

4.5.9 Making the appointments

It may not be necessary to make appointments for some of the roles this early in the project, e.g. Team Managers, Project Support, but there needs to be (as a minimum) a full understanding of the roles that will be required. Also, for external appointments (e.g. suppliers) it may not be possible to allocate roles if the activity to select the supplier (e.g. through tendering) is part of the project.

Appointees should be carefully matched to roles and fully briefed, both about the project and the PRINCE2 management framework, on joining the project. The expected time commitment should also be estimated and agreed. Ideally, role descriptions should be tailored specifically to the project in question.

In a well-run project, everybody involved in the management understands and agrees who is accountable, to whom and for what. Also, everyone is aware and familiar with the lines of communication.

The responsibilities of the Project Board members should be defined. Appendix C provides role description outlines for all the PRINCE2 roles – however, the generic role descriptions should always be tailored and specific to the particular project context.

4.6 PREPARE THE OUTLINE BUSINESS CASE

In project management it is all too easy to concentrate on what has to be done and how it should be done, while overlooking why it needs to be done. The Business Case defines why the work needs to be done and, as such, provides a crucial baseline for the project (see Figure 4.2).

In PRINCE2, the Business Case is developed at the beginning of the project and maintained throughout the life of the project, being formally verified by the Project Board at each key decision point, such as end stage assessments, and confirmed throughout the period that the benefits accrue. Note that the responsibility for confirming benefits post-project needs to be transferred from the Project Board to corporate or programme management when closing the project.

The Executive is responsible for the Business Case and therefore its development. This does not necessarily mean that the Executive writes the Business Case: the responsibility is to ensure that it is written and to underwrite its content. Preparing the Business Case may be delegated, for example, to a business analyst or to the Project Manager (if they possess the appropriate business skills).

Given the often relatively scarce information available at this point, the Business Case is likely to have a high-level perspective at this time, and will need to be refined during project initiation.

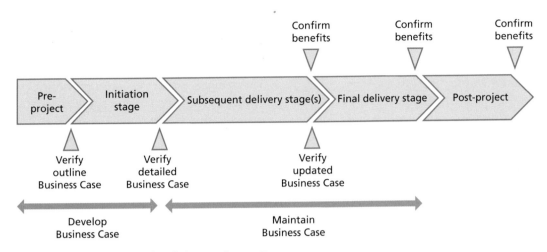

Figure 4.2 The development path of the Business Case

Nevertheless, sufficient time should be allowed for developing, reviewing and approving the outline Business Case because:

- It is the most important control in the project. It drives the decision-making processes and is used continually to align the project's progress to the business objectives and benefits that have been agreed
- It justifies the project effort, based on the estimated costs, the risks involved and the expected business benefits
- It covers the entire scope of business changes being introduced by the project (e.g. the cost of introducing new equipment should include the impact on personnel, training, changed procedures, accommodation changes, operational costs, relationships with the public etc.).

The outline Business Case is based on costs and timescales that are at best approximate. Once the costs and timescales are better understood, the viability may increase or decrease – perhaps resulting in the need to change the selected business option. Accordingly, it is often wise to consider the cost, benefit and risk appraisals for each option.

The information in the Business Case is necessary to assess the balance between the development, operational, maintenance and support costs against the financial value of the benefits over a period of time, in order to achieve an informed business commitment to the project. This is often termed an investment (or cost/benefit) appraisal and the figures are normally profiled over a fixed number of years, or the useful life of the project's products. Corporate or programme management may have prescribed accounting rules defining how the investment should be appraised.

The Project Board needs to ensure that the benefits cited are aligned to any related strategic and/or programme initiatives planned.

The baseline for investment appraisal is usually the 'do nothing' option, i.e. the picture of the likely costs and benefits if the project is not undertaken. If circumstances dictate that 'something must be done' (e.g. imminent new legislation), the baseline might instead be 'do the minimum'. Whichever baseline applies, it should be used for comparison with the expected outcome of the 'recommended' project option.

Wherever possible, benefits should be expressed in tangible ways. To start with, the customer, user or Executive may define many benefits as intangible – for example, 'happier staff'. For a large investment, benefits should be expressed in more tangible ways. In this example, 'happier staff' may translate into lower staff turnover and/or less time off for stress-related problems. Both of these can be converted into a likely financial saving.

A factor that often occurs when a project involves a commercial agreement between more than one organization is that the customer and supplier have independent Business Cases for the investment, reflecting their own business interests. In this case, the Executive must clarify and champion the Business Case on behalf of corporate or programme management.

4.7 PREPARE THE PROJECT BRIEF

A Project Brief is used to provide a full and firm foundation for the initiation of the project. Later, in the Initiating a Project process, the Project Manager extends and refines the contents of the Project Brief to create the Project Initiation Documentation, after which the Project Brief is no longer maintained.

The Project Manager will create the Project Brief on behalf of the Executive. Nevertheless, Project Board members are encouraged to be available for consultation and to provide guidance and support during this activity so that the completed Project Brief adequately summarizes their requirements and there are no surprises when it is submitted for approval.

The Project Brief comprises:

- **Project definition:** explaining what the project needs to achieve
- **Outline Business Case:** explaining why the project is needed and why the particular business option has been selected
- **Project Product Description:** providing customer quality expectations, user acceptance criteria and operations and maintenance acceptance criteria (see section 4.7.1)
- **Project approach:** defining the choice of solution the project will use to deliver the business option selected from the Business Case and taking into consideration the operational environment into which the solution must fit
- **Project management team structure:** a chart showing who will be involved with the project
- **Role descriptions:** describing the roles of the project management team and any other key resources identified at this time
- **References:** providing links to any associated documents or products.

4.7.1 The Project Product Description

The Project Product Description includes:

- The overall purpose of the project's outputs
- Its composition (i.e. the set of products it needs to comprise)
- The development skills required
- Customer's quality expectations (see section 4.7.2)

- Acceptance criteria, acceptance method and acceptance responsibilities (see section 4.7.3)
- Project-level quality tolerances.

The Project Product Description defines what the customer is expecting the project to deliver and the project approach defines the solution or method to be used by the supplier to create the Project Product.

4.7.2 The customer's quality expectations

The customer's quality expectations are captured in discussions with the customer, to avoid misinterpretations and inaccurate assumptions about the project's quality requirements. The customer's quality expectations should cover:

- The key quality requirements for the Project Product
- Any standards and processes that will need to be applied to achieve the specified quality requirements, including the extent to which the customer's quality management system (QMS) and/or supplier's QMS should be used
- Any measurements that may be useful to assess whether the Project Product meets the quality requirements – for example existing customer satisfaction measures.

The key quality requirements will drive the choice of solution and in turn influence the time, cost, scope, risk and benefit performance goals of the project.

> **Examples of quality expectation**
>
> The quality expectation for a water pump in a remote village is that it is robust enough to 'last a lifetime', whereas because the oil pump in a racing car needs to be as light as possible, it may only need to last the duration of one race.

The customer's quality expectations are often expressed in broad terms as a means to gain common understanding of general quality requirements. They are then used to identify more detailed acceptance criteria, which should be specific and precise.

Where possible, the customer's quality expectations should be prioritized as they will be used as inputs to define quality tolerances for the project's products.

The customer's quality expectations should be reviewed at the end of each management stage in case any factors external to the project have changed them.

4.7.3 Acceptance criteria

The project's acceptance criteria form a prioritized list of measurable definitions of the attributes that must apply to the set of products to be acceptable to key stakeholders. Examples are ease of use, ease of support, ease of maintenance, appearance, major functions, development costs, running costs, capacity, availability, reliability, security, accuracy and performance.

Acceptance criteria should be prioritized as this helps if there has to be a trade-off between some criteria. High quality, early delivery and low cost, for example, may not be compatible and one of them may need to be sacrificed in order to achieve the other two.

> **Example of a prioritization technique – MoSCoW**
>
> Each acceptance criterion is rated as either Must have, Should have, Could have or Won't have for now.
>
> All the 'Must Have' and 'Should have' acceptance criteria should be mutually achievable.

When the project can demonstrate that all the acceptance criteria have been met, the project's obligations are fulfilled and the project can be closed.

It is important to recognize that little may be understood about the project's products at this early stage. Consequently, it is often the case that acceptance criteria will be refined and agreed during the Initiating a Project process and reviewed at the end of each management stage. Once finalized in the Project Product Description, acceptance criteria are subject to change control and should only be changed with the approval of the Project Board.

In considering acceptance criteria, it is useful to select proxy measures that will be accurate and reliable indicators as to whether business benefits will be achieved subsequently.

> **Example of acceptance criteria**
>
> If a customer's quality expectation for a water pump is that it 'lasts a lifetime', the acceptance criteria should focus on those measures that provide sufficient indication or confidence that the pump is capable of lasting a lifetime (defined as a specific number of years). This may include complying with certain engineering standards relating to product durability.

Identifying the acceptance methods is crucial because they address the question 'How do we prove whether and when the project product has been completed and is acceptable to the customer?'

4.8 PREPARE THE INITIATION STAGE PLAN

The Project Manager prepares the Initiation Stage Plan with any necessary support from Project Board members.

The temptation to put pressure on the Project Manager to complete initiation quickly should be resisted where possible, as a rushed initiation will often lead to a poor project subsequently. Project Board members should be careful not to underestimate the effort required to initiate a project properly and provide the Project Manager with sufficient resource and time accordingly.

Generally, the effort required to initiate a project should be in proportion to the scale and business priority of the project concerned.

4.9 STARTING UP A PROJECT: SUMMARY

PRINCE2 is not specific about who undertakes the Starting up a Project process activities because the project does not exist officially until the Project Board authorizes the initiation stage (see Chapter 5).

The following are the recommended actions that the Executive needs either to undertake, delegate or arrange for with corporate or programme management.

Recommended actions for Starting up a Project

Confirm the understanding of the project:

- Review the project mandate and obtain any missing information.

Corporate/programme Manager to appoint the Executive and the Executive to appoint the Project Manager:

- Identify the candidates and responsibilities for the Executive and Project Manager
- Confirm the selected people's availability, their acceptance of these roles and their commitment to carry them out
- Prepare role descriptions for the Executive and Project Manager and confirm appointments with corporate or programme management.

Incorporate lessons learned:

- Review related End Project Reports and Lessons Reports from similar projects (whether internally or externally) to identify lessons which can be applied to this project.

Design and appoint the project management team:

- Identify candidates for remaining project management team roles and create role descriptions
- Assess whether any members of the Project Board are likely to delegate any of their assurance responsibilities to a Project Assurance role
- Consider whether the Project Manager will also fulfil the Team Manager(s) and Project Support roles or whether the separate individuals will be filling these roles
- Appoint identified individuals to the roles of Senior Supplier(s), Senior User(s), Project Assurance (where appropriate), Project Support (where appropriate) and Team Managers (where appropriate)
- Ensure that these individuals understand and are actively committed to carrying out their roles and responsibilities in the management and support of the project
- Confirm the reporting and communication lines.

Prepare the outline Business Case:

- Assemble any relevant background information, e.g. contracts, feasibility reports, service level agreements, alignment to corporate or programme strategy etc.
- Determine the approximate cost/benefit for the project
- Draft the Business Case in the light of what is now known about the project; this is likely to be incomplete at this time.

Prepare the project approach and assemble the Project Brief:

- Assist and advise the Project Manager in devising the project approach and assembling the Project Brief.

Plan the initiation stage:

- Assist and advise the Project Manager during the preparation of the Initiation Stage Plan.

Authorize initiation

5 Authorize initiation

Purpose

The purpose of authorizing initiation is to decide whether it is a worthwhile investment to develop the outline Business Case further by initiating a formal project. The Project Board decides whether to proceed by assessing the Project Brief. If the decision is to proceed, the Project Board must review and approve the Stage Plan for the initiation stage.

What to expect from the Project Manager

At this point, Project Board members should have been working closely with the Project Manager (during Starting up a Project – see Chapter 4) to prepare for this decision, so there should be no surprises. The Project Manager assembles the Project Brief and the Initiation Stage Plan and submits them for approval.

5.1 CONTEXT

In Chapter 4 we described how, in the Starting up a Project process, the project management team is appointed and the outline Business Case is developed; also, how the Project Brief and Initiation Stage Plan are developed by the Project Manager.

Authorizing initiation is the first activity in the Directing a Project process and covers the Project Board's activities to review and approve the outline Business Case, Project Brief and Stage Plan.

The purpose of authorizing initiation is to check the viability, desirability and achievability of the project before committing funds and resources to initiate it. Towards the end of Starting up a Project,

the Project Manager will request authorization for the funds and resources required to initiate the project. The Project Board members consider the authorization based on two documents, the Project Brief and the Initiation Stage Plan (see Figure 5.1).

It is important to understand that, at this point, the Project Board is only authorizing the work of project initiation. The project as a whole is not being authorized. In practical financial terms, this may mean that the likelihood of the project, and a provisional budget, may have been agreed – but it is only the funding for the initiation stage that is being released to the Project Manager.

5.1.1 What is the Project Brief?

The purpose of the Project Brief is to make sure that there is a common understanding of the business purposes of the project, its scope, the risks involved, and its likely governance requirements before detailed project planning gets under way in the initiation stage.

Reviewing and approving/rejecting the Project Brief helps to counter the first of two major project management **risks** at this point – **that the wrong project will be planned.**

5.1.2 What is the Initiation Stage Plan?

Also at this point, the Project Manager submits a Stage Plan for the initiation stage, a mandatory stage in PRINCE2. The Initiation Stage Plan not only communicates the necessary management and planning activities required during initiation, but also counters the second of the two major project management **risks** – that **the planning activity during initiation may, itself, run out of control.**

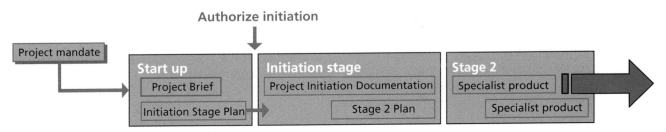

Figure 5.1 Authorize initiation

The project's stakeholders (business, user and supplier interests) may still have markedly different views on the detailed approach to be adopted or the solution required. This can lead to protracted debates, false starts, impasses and/or uncertain commitment. The control framework included with the Initiation Stage Plan will ensure that any loss of momentum is highlighted and managed.

5.2 APPROVE THE PROJECT BRIEF

5.2.1 Overview

A Product Description for the Project Brief is provided (in Appendix A) and this includes some generic quality criteria against which the Project Brief should be assessed. It is good practice to add in other, more specific criteria relating to the project in question.

The Project Brief should be concise. Its purpose is to avoid time being wasted on detailed planning before there is adequate agreement on what the project is about and whether it is a worthwhile business investment – so it would defeat this purpose if the Project Manager were to waste time instead producing a voluminous Project Brief. Some information may not be available (or agreed) at this early point. What is important is that sufficient information is agreed for the detailed planning to commence.

The Project Manager will have worked informally with Project Board members on the content of the Project Brief – this is encouraged and Project Board members should make every effort to be available for the purpose (see section 4.7).

The evolving outline Business Case, in particular, should be monitored carefully by the Project Board. Clearly, if it becomes evident that the project is not viable, whether because of flaws in the proposed initiative or other business priorities, it may be considered that continuing work on initiating the project is pointless.

5.2.2 Areas of focus

Broadly speaking, the Executive will be most concerned with the validity of the outline Business Case. An important aspect of this is that the Business Case should be aligned to relevant corporate strategies and investment priorities. A project with a perfectly healthy Business Case may

not be a good candidate for investment if there are other business priorities at the time.

Senior Users will be concerned with the business benefits, because they will have the long-term responsibility for realizing them. Senior Users will also wish to ensure that the customer's quality expectations and acceptance criteria have been properly represented in the Project Brief. The Brief contains a Project Product Description which should be a concise but accurate description of what the project will deliver.

The Senior Supplier's focus will be on the project approach (is it feasible?) and scope (what do they need to deliver?). Important considerations will be whether key assumptions and dependencies have been identified and the extent to which they need to be regarded and managed as risks.

The proposals for the structure and appointments for the project management team should be carefully considered by all Project Board members. Those involved in the project's management need to have the experience, knowledge and authority appropriate for the scale and nature of the project – also the personal qualities to be able to work together effectively as a team.

5.2.3 Achieving agreement

Ultimately, the Project Board members, as a team, need to review and approve the Project Brief as a whole, to ensure there is a sound, common understanding. An efficient way to achieve this (for any important document) is to employ a structured quality inspection or review technique – with a meeting or a telephone conference. The *Managing Successful Projects with PRINCE2* manual describes a simple, generic quality review technique of this type. Techniques such as this provide a systematic and efficient way to facilitate agreement and resolve errors, omissions and ambiguities.

5.3 APPROVE THE INITIATION STAGE PLAN

5.3.1 Plan presentation

In PRINCE2, the plans submitted to the Project Board should all have a consistent format, i.e. in terms of plan components. The consistent format assists in communication and becomes familiar, both to the Project Manager (who understands what to produce) and to Project Board members (who know what to look for and where to find it). A Product Description for a plan is supplied (in Appendix A) including some generic quality criteria against which the plan should be assessed.

The level of formality in the documentation may vary from project to project according to the scale of the project and the business risks. On simple projects, for example, a set of slides may be sufficient. Project Board members should decide on an appropriate level of formality in consultation with the Project Manager.

5.3.2 Implications of approving the Initiation Stage Plan

The Project Board authorizes initiation by approving the Initiation Stage Plan. Depending on the level of formality agreed, members may or may not meet for the purpose. However, it is essential that all Project Board members approve the plan and understand that, by doing so, they are:

- Endorsing the effort and costs involved
- (Most importantly) committing to make the necessary resources available.

Initiating the project will involve the Project Manager:

- Developing and assembling the components of a Project Initiation Documentation
- Producing a Stage Plan for the succeeding management stage – i.e. when the 'delivery' or 'execution' work will commence.

From discussions with the Project Manager and other knowledgeable stakeholders (e.g. Project Assurance personnel or programme-level managers), Project Board members should satisfy themselves that the plan is sound. The Project Board may decide to approve the plan with or without modifications.

One of the key objectives of the Initiation Stage Plan is to ensure that initiation work remains under control. Project Board members should also review and approve the reporting and control mechanisms. Finally, the Project Board should confirm the tolerances for the initiation stage. Tolerances are introduced in section 3.3.2 (Project Board duties and behaviours) and provide the Project Manager with a defined measure of discretion before decisions have to be escalated to the Project Board.

5.4 COMMUNICATION

The Project Board's duty to lead communication and set expectations is never more crucial than during initiation. At this point, the approach and plans often evolve rapidly or change abruptly, so care should be taken to manage expectations and avoid making premature commitments.

At this early point, there will not be an agreed Communications Management Strategy for the project (though there may be one at programme level), but effective communication is nevertheless vital. This is especially important for clarifying business objectives and project scope with the programme or corporate managers who are commissioning the project.

The work of initiating a project may take anything from a single day to several months depending on a number of factors.

5.5 SUGGESTED PROJECT BOARD AGENDA

A generic agenda for Project Board reviews was introduced in Chapter 3 (section 3.6.1). The specific implementation suggested for authorizing initiation is outlined below.

> **Suggested Project Board agenda for authorizing initiation**
>
> **1 Look back**
>
> Review the background to the project and the Project Brief
>
> **2 Look forward**
>
> Preview the Initiation Stage Plan
>
> **3 Assess overall project viability**
>
> Review the outline Business Case and key issues/ risks
>
> **4 Make a decision**
>
> Authorize the initiation stage to commence (by approving the Initiation Stage Plan and Project Brief).

5.6 AUTHORIZE INITIATION: SUMMARY

PRINCE2 requires that Project Board members undertake the following responsibilities collectively for authorizing initiation.

Actions required for authorizing initiation

Review and approve the Project Brief:

- Confirm the project definition and approach
- Review and approve the Project Product Description
- Formally confirm the appointments to the core project management team
- Review and approve the outline Business Case, particularly the projected business benefits.

Approve the Initiation Stage Plan:

- Approve the plan to develop the Project Initiation Documentation
- Obtain or commit the resources needed by the Stage Plan for the initiation stage
- Ensure that adequate reporting and control mechanisms are in place for the initiation stage
- Set tolerances for the initiation stage
- Request the necessary logistical support (for example accommodation, communication facilities, equipment and any Project Support) from corporate or programme management
- Understand any risks that affect the decision to authorize initiation
- Confirm to the Project Manager that the work defined in the Initiation Stage Plan may start.

Communicate:

- Keep stakeholders (corporate or programme management and other interested parties) informed about project progress by issuing a project initiation notification.

Authorize the project 6

6 Authorize the project

Purpose

The purpose of authorizing the project is to decide whether to commit to the project as a business investment. The decision is based on detailed Project Initiation Documentation which has been developed by the project management team from the Project Brief. Once the Project Initiation Documentation has been approved by the Project Board, it becomes the baseline for all forms of project control, covering project benefits, risks, scope, quality requirements, costs and timescales. Members of the Project Board can then go on to consider and approve the Stage Plan for the stage that follows initiation (see Chapter 7), and approval is often achieved at the same Project Board review.

What to expect from the Project Manager

Initiation is a crucial stage, consisting entirely of management preparations for the project. In the course of initiation, it is normal for the Project Manager to seek regular guidance from Project Board members (see Chapter 8). Consequently, when the Project Manager introduces the Project Initiation Documentation for approval, there should, again, be no surprises.

6.1 CONTEXT

The decision whether to authorize the overall project is taken by Project Board members at the end of the initiation stage (see Figure 6.1). The initiation stage consists of project management activity, mostly planning, and takes place before the specialist project delivery (or 'execution') activities commence.

The purpose of initiation is to agree the answers to a number of crucial questions about the investment and work being embarked upon – and these are addressed in the following sections. It is only when the answers to these questions have been agreed that the Project Board members can authorize the project consistent with their duty to provide unified direction.

6.1.1 Why?

Why do we want to undertake the project? There must be some benefits. What will they be? Who will gain the benefits? What will be the value of the benefits? How will we know that they have been achieved and how will we measure them?

On the other hand, what will be the costs? Might they outweigh the benefits? What about the uncertainties? Are the business risks worthwhile?

All these questions must be resolved in the project's Business Case and supported by a risk assessment. At the beginning of project initiation, the Business Case may or may not be clear, but by the time the Project Board authorizes the project, members must have a clear, common understanding of the business justification for the project. The Business Case is then updated and monitored throughout the project, acting as the key Project Board control – consistent with the PRINCE2 principle that a project must have continued business justification.

It is easy to assume that merely by delivering the products of the project the benefits will be realized, but this is often not the case. The realization of benefits needs to be actively managed and monitored. If the project is part of a programme, benefits management may be handled entirely at programme level. If not, it is wise to include a Benefits Review Plan alongside the

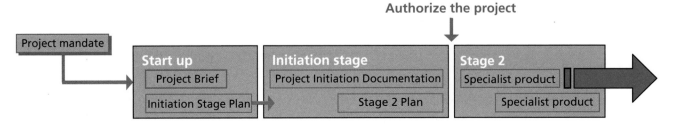

Figure 6.1 Authorize the project

Business Case to ensure that the target benefits are managed and achieved, whether this starts during the project or after project completion.

6.1.2 What?

What does the project deed to deliver? Another PRINCE2 principle is that the focus of project work must be on its products and on product quality. In project work, there is no point in any activity unless it contributes to a product. Consequently, focusing on the products provides us with the best means of clarifying the scope of the project.

The products' quality criteria also have an impact on activities, in that these determine the nature and extent of the quality controls that need to be applied. For example, project X may be generating the same type of products as project Y but project X may require an urgent, short-term solution whereas project Y is required to implement a robust long-term solution – the activities, products and quality controls are likely to be very different.

PRINCE2 requires a Quality Management Strategy and a set of Product Descriptions (with project-specific quality criteria). These management products pin down exactly what the project will create and are derived from the Project Product Description which was included in the Project Brief.

6.1.3 How?

The Quality Management Strategy outlines the key methods, techniques and tools to be used and specifies any standards that must be observed. It is supported by a Configuration Management Strategy, describing how the products of the project will be stored and controlled, e.g. in terms of naming standards, version control, baselines and detailed change control.

The specialist aspects of developing the project products are summarized in the project approach and in the Product Descriptions. The Product Descriptions contain the details of quality methods to be used in developing and checking each of the products.

Deciding on the specialist technical approach is not all, though. There must also be a thorough understanding of how the work will be controlled. PRINCE2 provides all the generic controls required but these must be tailored to the needs of the specific project – the project controls are documented in the Project Initiation Documentation. Where similar types of project are

conducted frequently by an organization, it is good practice to undertake measurement and analysis of project performance for the purposes of continual improvement. Aspects of performance that organizations may wish to analyse are discussed in Chapter 9, section 9.3.1. Arrangements for project controls should therefore include details of any measurements that must be collected in the course of monitoring.

6.1.4 Who?

Who will be the key players in the project management team? The Project Board members, Project Manager, Team Managers? How will the Project Assurance function be fulfilled? What kind of Project Support will be required?

Some of these appointments have already been agreed in the course of Starting up a Project (Chapter 4) but it is not unusual for there to be changes during initiation. Provision may also have to be made for participants who may join the project later on, such as external suppliers.

The project management team structure, roles and responsibilities have to be defined and agreed with the personnel concerned as part of project initiation.

6.1.5 How much?

With the approach defined, the planners can establish the resourcing required for the project, the availability of those resources and, ultimately, estimate the costs. These are laid out in resourcing and finance sections of the Project Plan.

6.1.6 When?

The effort then needs to be profiled over time, taking into account the availability of resources, the dependencies between the products and any external dependencies (products that are 'out of scope' but nevertheless needed for the project to be completed). The timing of the key activities and products is summarized in the Project Plan.

6.1.7 Are the risks acceptable?

A Risk Management Strategy needs to be agreed.

The risks identified at this point need to be managed as the work progresses and new risks start to emerge. To help manage risks, a Risk Register needs to be established that identifies each risk and the recommended risk responses. PRINCE2 recommends using one or more of a number of risk responses as shown in Figure 6.2.

Threat responses	Opportunity responses
Avoid	Exploit
Reduce (probability and/or impact) Fallback (reduces impact only) Transfer (reduces impact only, and often only the financial impact)	Enhance
Share	
Accept	Reject

Figure 6.2 Threat and opportunity responses

6.1.8 What should we tell people?

Lastly, the project management team needs to agree how best to communicate its objectives and progress – both internally and with key external stakeholders. A suitable Communication Management Strategy is prepared for this purpose.

6.1.9 Are we ready to start?

In PRINCE2, all the decisions, plans and strategies used to answer the fundamental questions posed above become components of the Project Initiation Documentation. The Project Initiation Documentation is the baseline for all subsequent management control (replacing the Project Brief).

Of course, some of the components of the Project Initiation Documentation may need to be changed as the work progresses – but once the Project Initiation Documentation is approved, change proposals will be subject to strict change controls implemented by the Project Manager. Any significant proposal relating to the Project Initiation Documentation must be referred to the Project Board for a decision.

The Project Initiation Documentation has to be agreed and approved to authorize the project and this is perhaps the most important decision Project Board members will have to make.

In order for the specialist work to commence, however, the Stage Plan for the first management stage must also be approved (see Chapter 7). Approving these two management products – the Project Initiation Documentation and the Stage Plan for the next stage – provides the trigger for 'delivery' (or 'execution') to begin.

6.1.10 Have we established the right level of governance?

A key consideration is how much governance the project merits. In determining this, it can help to consider whether the project is 'simple', 'typical' or 'daunting'. Indeed, there may really be more than one project – the scale and nature of the change may warrant setting up a programme. Such considerations are highlighted in Table 6.1.

There are a number of clues to look for as to whether the initiative is best managed as a programme:

- Are there several markedly different specialist work-streams involved?
- Will the project require dedicated functions for quality assurance, configuration management, contract management, financial management or, especially, benefits management?

Table 6.1 Examples of projects of different scales

Project scale		Characteristic	Applying PRINCE2
High ↑ ... Low ↓	Programme	Business transformation	A programme management framework such as OGC's *Managing Successful Programmes* should be used. PRINCE2 may be used to manage projects within the programme.
	Daunting project	High risk, cost, importance, visibility Multiple organizations Multi-disciplinary (e.g. construction, IT and business change) International	Multiple delivery stages Extended Project Board (e.g. user/supplier groups) Team Managers as a separate role likely Project Support as a separate role likely Individual management products
	Normal project	Medium risk, cost, importance, visibility Commercial customer/supplier relationship Multiple sites	One or more delivery stages Standard Project Board Team Managers as a separate role optional Project Support as a separate role optional Some management products combined
	Simple project	Low risk, cost, importance, visibility Single organization Single site	Single delivery stage Simple Project Board The Project Manager fulfils the Team Manager role The Project Manager fulfils the Project Support role Combined management products
	Task	If there is a single-person Project Board (and typically the Executive is the Project Manager's line manager) then it could normally be treated as a task. The Project Manager may also be the person doing the work. The costs may be within the 'business as usual' budget. Straightforward business justification – e.g. responding to an instruction.	Treat as a Work Package that delivers one or more products. Use Work Packages, Product Descriptions, Logs/Registers and Checkpoint Reports.

- Are the products required of the project likely to become clear during initiation or will they still be only vaguely defined?
- Are there several autonomous businesses/organizations involved?
- Will stakeholders in different locations be impacted in markedly different ways?

PRINCE2 is very flexible, and it should be stressed that none of these questions will necessarily provide a definitive answer to the question 'Is it a task, a project or a programme?', but selecting the correct form of governance, particularly for a large-scale change, is immensely important. It is much better to address the question at this point than to discover, later, that the provision made for managing the effort is too much or inadequate.

6.2 COMMUNICATION

6.2.1 Consultations and informal approvals

For a project of any appreciable size, the Initiating a Project process involves many decisions and a considerable amount of work. It makes no sense for Project Board members to stand back and wait for completed Project Initiation Documentation to be submitted. The Project Manager and others involved in planning must have confidence that the evolving plans are based on an accurate understanding of the Project Board's wishes and objectives. It is essential that Project Board members are available for consultation, and that members' informal approvals of the emerging strategies and plans are carefully considered. The aim should be that there are no surprises when the Project Initiation Documentation is finally assembled and submitted.

If Project Board members fail to communicate effectively – with each other and/or with the Project Manager and others involved in planning – initiation can be fraught with false starts, disagreements, waste and rework, getting the project off to a poor start, with obvious effects on morale.

It is really only after the project has been authorized that the Project Board members can begin managing by exception.

6.2.2 Initiation workshops

Workshops or 'kick-off meetings' can be very useful during project start-up and initiation. They help with team-building and exchanging viewpoints, not least about the best way to tailor PRINCE2.

Documentation templates may be useful as a means to record information and decisions thoroughly and consistently, but they cannot simply be 'filled out' to create a plan.

Sound initiation requires extensive communication, and workshops are a speedy and efficient use of time. Project Board members should give priority, wherever possible, to attending. Project initiation (or definition) workshops may be focused on defining the roles and responsibilities of participants in the project management team and/or on project scope and approach (where PRINCE2's product-based planning technique can be exceptionally useful for communication purposes).

6.2.3 Allow time for planning

Project Board members should resist the temptation to pressurize the Project Manager into submitting plans quickly – unless there are really legitimate reasons for doing so. Projects are frequently labelled 'urgent' simply as a form of motivation to get things done quickly or to please the customer with a rapid response. All too often this leads to:

- Poor planning
- Unrealistic expectations
- Project activities rushed in an attempt to meet the planned timescales
- Quality problems
- High volumes of change
- Failure.

If the pressures on time really are valid, say to meet a legislative deadline, Project Board members should encourage the Project Manager to highlight the attendant risks in plans and, where possible, formulate effective countermeasures. This approach results in a more mature dialogue with customers and users and a potentially better business relationship.

6.3 REVIEW THE END STAGE REPORT FOR INITIATION

If the context enabled initiation to be completed in just a few days, this might be a relatively trivial task. On the other hand, initiating a large project can take several weeks or even months, and in these circumstances it is crucial to confirm that the stage was completed within tolerances and to assess how

7 Authorize a Stage or Exception Plan

Purpose

Once the project has been authorized (and the Project Initiation Documentation approved), the project progresses as a series of one or more delivery stages, during which the products of the project are created. Authorizing a Stage or Exception Plan is the activity performed by the Project Board at each 'stage boundary'. This activity is also performed by the Project Board in the event of an exception that results in an Exception Plan being produced and submitted for approval. An exception is a condition occurring during a stage which requires escalation to the Project Board, because it prevents the Project Manager from completing the stage within agreed tolerances.

The purpose of authorizing a Stage or Exception Plan is to provide the Project Board with an opportunity to review progress, reaffirm the business viability of the project and give the Project Manager approval to proceed based on an agreed plan (i.e. either the next Stage Plan or an Exception Plan for the current stage).

What to expect from the Project Manager

When authorizing a Stage (or Exception) Plan, Project Board members should expect the Project Manager to provide an End Stage Report (or Exception Report) describing current project progress (notably the status of the products, the budget, any benefits and/or risks and, in the case of an exception, the planning options considered for recovery).

Project Board members should additionally be confident that the project's plans and records are being properly maintained. The Project Manager should submit a suitably detailed Stage Plan for the next stage (or an Exception Plan, if applicable).

If the Stage Plan is for the final stage, Project Board members should ensure that the PRINCE2 project closure activities are incorporated into the Stage Plan.

7.1 CONTEXT

Once the Project Initiation Documentation and the Project Plan have been approved, the project proceeds as a series of management stages, with Stage Plans acting as notional contracts between the Project Board and the Project Manager.

7.1.1 Stage boundaries

Although Project Board members should continue to provide ad hoc direction as necessary (see Chapter 8), the aim, for the most part, is for them to 'manage by exception'.

This means that the Project Board's contribution is focused on key control points (stage boundaries – see Figure 7.1) when:

- Progress in relation to the current stage contract and the overall project is reported and reviewed (in an End Stage Report)
- A Stage Plan 'contract' for the next stage is established.

Figure 7.2 illustrates the typical profile of Project Board activity in a PRINCE2 project. Note that the effort is heavily 'front-loaded', with peak activity during project initiation. Thereafter, there should be smaller peaks at stage boundaries and minor blips during the stages (perhaps for reacting to Highlight Reports or Issue Reports). There is also likely to be another peak as the project's products are handed over for use. This pattern will of course be different if the handover of products for operational use is phased in some way.

Projects that do not have front-loaded involvement of the Project Board tend to have a profile showing greater and more haphazard involvement at later stages through an increased need for Project Board interventions or consultations.

7.1.2 Exceptions

Nevertheless, even in a well-managed project, it has to be accepted that project work is inherently risky and things will not always go to plan. PRINCE2 accommodates this by including a simple process for managing 'exceptions'. An exception occurs when, for whatever reason, it is forecast that a stage is

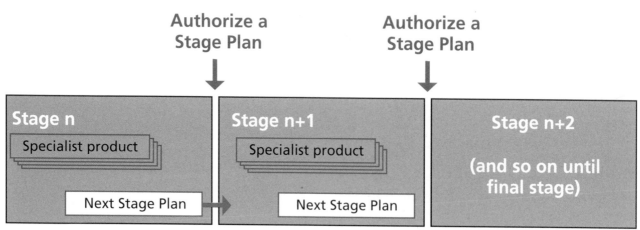

Figure 7.1 Authorize a Stage Plan

unlikely to be completed within agreed tolerances (see Figure 7.3) or that the project overall will not complete within the tolerances approved by corporate or programme management.

In the course of their regular progress monitoring, Project Managers continually update forecasts for the cost and duration of a stage (and the project). Potential exceptions are often identified as a result of this monitoring. Other sources of exceptions may be problems or concerns, important change requests, off-specifications or a combination of increasing risks.

Moreover, an impending exception may become apparent to Project Board members before it is recognized by the Project Manager, e.g. as a result of board members' wider awareness of the business environment surrounding the project.

Normally, the first step in the exception process is for the Project Manager to prepare an

Exception Report outlining the nature of the exception, any options for responding to it and a recommendation.

Chapter 8 describes the ways in which the Project Board can respond to an Exception Report (see section 8.3.2), one of which is to request an Exception Plan.

7.1.3 Project Board meetings

PRINCE2 does not mandate a particular level of formality for documentation or meetings. However, granting an 'approval to proceed' is an important ('go/no go') decision that should be made collectively by the Project Board members – the Executive is ultimately accountable but the principle holds that all three interests (business, user and supplier) must be satisfied to achieve success. In most circumstances, this implies a meeting of some sort. Telephone or video

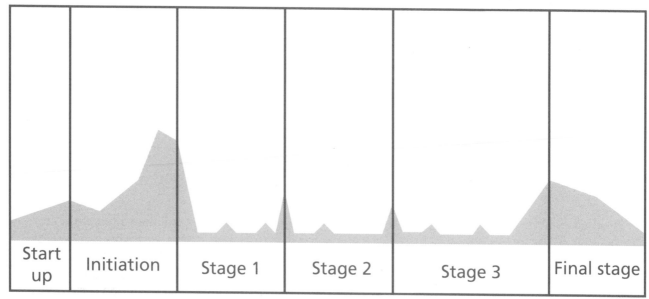

Figure 7.2 Managing by exception – profile of Project Board effort

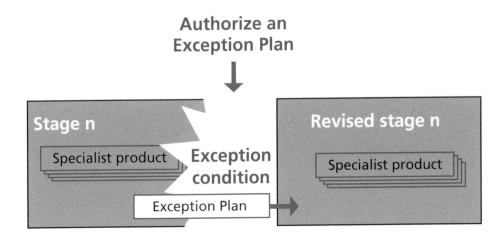

Figure 7.3 Authorize an Exception Plan

conferences are valid options if it is difficult to convene physically.

Deciding whether and how to meet – and the level of formality – should be based on the amount of business risk the project involves. Remember, also, that this is an opportunity to demonstrate commitment, both to the project management team and to the wider organization.

If some form of meeting is convened, Project Board members should attend with the Project Manager. Administrative support may be supplied by someone from the Project Support function, and personnel with Project Assurance responsibilities may also attend.

Other personnel can be invited – whether to observe or to provide expert advice – but it is the Project Board members who make the decisions. A suggested outline agenda is given in section 7.5.

It is important that Project Board reviews focus on plans – reviewing progress in relation to plans and approving the implementation of plans. PRINCE2 employs plans as notional contracts between the Project Board and the Project Manager. Project Board meetings are not talking shops. It can quickly be apparent when a project is beginning to run out of control – the Project Board meetings tend to turn into 'issue reviews', focusing on fire-fighting the latest problems. If this persists, and the meetings lose the necessary focus on plans, the project is no longer using PRINCE2 – it is out of control.

The Project Board's approach and decision making for stage boundaries (authorizing a Stage Plan) and exceptions (authorizing an Exception Plan) are

remarkably similar, and the decisions themselves are essentially the same.

7.2 REVIEW END STAGE REPORTS

The current stage is not formally complete until the Project Board accepts it as such.

The Project Manager's End Stage Report may take the form of a document, a slide presentation or even a verbal account – whichever is agreed as suitable.

What Project Board members want to know is:

■ Are all the stage products complete?
■ Have they met their respective quality criteria? Were they assessed by appropriate quality authorities?
■ If there are any activities which span the stage boundary, are they on track?
■ Were there any benefits reviews? What is the status of any benefits due to be realized during the stage?
■ Were there any significant issues during the stage? How were they dealt with? What were the root causes and corrective actions?
■ Was the work completed within budget and schedule tolerances or within any other tolerances that were set, e.g. scope or quality constraints?
■ Have we learned any important lessons during the stage? (A Lessons Report may be included with the End Stage Report.)

The Project Manager should be able to back up the report with evidence from progress records, from the Quality Register, Issue Register, Lessons

Log and the Risk Register. Project Assurance and/or Project Support personnel may also be able to help confirm the detail.

Some loose ends may be acceptable. For instance, a minor product may be incomplete or quality review/testing follow-up action on a major product may not be fully resolved. The Project Board must judge the extent to which incomplete work represents a risk, but there are simple ways of managing minor slippages like these (see section 7.4).

However, if Project Board members are not satisfied that the stage is really complete, the Project Manager has not properly fulfilled the stage contract and Project Board members should make it clear that, in these circumstances, they expect to receive earlier warning in the form of an Exception Report – just pressing on, hoping that the situation can be recovered, is not an adequate response.

7.3 APPROVE STAGE OR EXCEPTION PLANS

7.3.1 Prior consultation and informal approval

Project Board members should always be available for consultation during the planning activity and take opportunities to give informal or provisional approval of the Stage Plan or Exception Plan before it is formally submitted.

If Project Board members fail to communicate effectively – with each other and/or with the Project Manager and others involved in planning – delays and uncertainty can arise both during plan preparation and in approval. On the other hand, if communication has been effective there will be no surprises when the plan is finally submitted and the Project Manager requests approval to proceed.

Note that, for simple exceptions, an Exception Plan can take the form of a simple request for change to the current Stage Plan. For instance, if the problem is a simple delay or need for additional budget, and there are no reasons to change other aspects of the plan, then a request for change is probably the most economic way forward. However, the request for change still effectively acts as an Exception Plan and must be treated as such, so that

its effects on the tolerances and Business Case are properly managed.

If the plan being reviewed is for the final stage of the project, Project Board members must ensure that it includes provision for all necessary project closure activities, including those outlined in the Closing a Project process (see Chapter 9 for a summary of these activities).

Project Board members should be satisfied that:

- The products are valid
- The assumptions are realistic
- The external dependencies will be satisfied
- The risks have been identified and suitable countermeasures planned
- The resourcing is adequate
- The resources are available and will be committed
- The timescales are realistic
- The quality criteria and methods proposed are appropriate
- The arrangements for monitoring, control and reporting are appropriate.

Although all Project Board members should consider, and have confidence in, all aspects of the Stage Plan or Exception Plan, each member will have a specific area of focus – and there are some cases where it is essential that there is a shared understanding. The following sections explore this in more detail.

7.3.1.1 Areas of shared focus

- Do the Product Descriptions accurately reflect the scope agreed for the stage?
- Does the Stage Plan accurately reflect the approach agreed for the stage (or for the agreed recovery action)?
- Can the Project Board commit to delivering all the necessary resources?
- Are the timescales and costs for the stage broadly in line with the Project Plan?
- Have the lessons learned from the earlier work (and other, similar projects) been properly taken into account in the plan (particularly if there has been an exception)?

7.3.1.2 The Executive's focus

- Are there any significant vulnerabilities in the plan?

- Have they been identified as risks?
- Are they manageable?
- Is it clear how they are to be managed?
- Is the framework of controls appropriate?
  - Is PRINCE2 being scaled and tailored sensibly?
  - If there has been an exception, should the pattern of controls and tolerances be changed to reduce the likelihood of further exceptions?

7.3.1.3 The Senior User's focus

- Are the planning assumptions relating to user resources and products realistic?
- Is there confidence that user-related dependencies (internal and external) will be met, e.g. customer obligations?
- Are the important risks for operational users identified accurately? Is it clear how they are to be managed?
- Will the Project Assurance arrangements adequately safeguard the interests of user stakeholders?
- Will users be adequately represented in quality control activities, e.g. as quality reviewers?
- Can the user personnel (and any other user resources) be committed to the project work as indicated in the plan?
- Is the timing of the user-related activity in the plan achievable bearing in mind business-as-usual commitments and any other parallel initiatives?
- Are the service functions and personnel who will be responsible for supporting and/or maintaining the specialist products after the project has delivered them adequately represented in the plan?
- What is the status of any benefits due to be realized at this point?

7.3.1.4 The Senior Supplier's focus

- Are the planning assumptions relating to specialist resources and products realistic?
- Is there confidence that specialist technical dependencies (internal and external) will be met, e.g. contractor and third-party supplier dependencies?
- Are appropriate technical methods, techniques, tools and standards being applied?

- Are the important technical risks identified accurately? Are they manageable? Is it clear how they will be managed?
- Will the current Project Assurance arrangements adequately safeguard the quality of the specialist technical effort?
- Will specialists be adequately represented in quality control activities, e.g. as quality reviewers?
- Will the Project Manager have sufficient technical support, e.g. for advice and guidance on specialist issues?
- Are people with the required specialist skills and experience available?
- Are the service functions and personnel who will be responsible for supporting and/or maintaining the specialist products after the project has delivered them adequately represented in the plan?
- Can the specialist personnel be committed to the project work as indicated in the plans? Can all the other specialist technical resources, such as equipment, be delivered?

7.3.2 Approve a Stage Plan

If the Project Board is authorizing a stage, there are two key decisions involved:

- Is the current stage complete?
- Do we progress on the basis of the plan for the next stage?

If Project Board members are happy on both counts, then they simply grant the authorization to proceed by approving the Stage Plan. In practice, there may be some concerns about progress – perhaps there is some work outstanding from the current stage or the Project Board is not fully confident of the plan for the next stage.

If these are just minor loose ends and the Project Board is confident they will be managed properly going forward, Project Board members may agree to grant conditional approval to proceed by either:

- Requiring the Project Manager to produce a Highlight Report, by a specific date, to confirm that the matters outstanding from the earlier stage have been resolved, or
- Requiring specific modifications to the plan for the next stage.

7.6 AUTHORIZE A STAGE OR EXCEPTION PLAN: SUMMARY

PRINCE2 requires that Project Board members undertake the following responsibilities collectively to authorize a Stage or Exception Plan.

Actions required for authorizing a Stage or Exception Plan

Review the End Stage Report (or Exception Report):

- If this is the end of a management stage, then review the performance status of the project using the End Stage Report for the current management stage. Include consideration of any benefits achieved or lessons learned during the stage

- If there is an exception, then review the status of the project and the background to the exception using the Exception Report.

Review and approve the next Stage Plan or Exception Plan:

- Review the plan for which the Project Manager is seeking approval (this will be a Stage Plan for the next management stage or an Exception Plan)

- Set the tolerances for the next management stage or (in the case of an Exception Plan) revise the current stage tolerances if necessary.

Assess overall project viability:

- Review the Project Plan and the position in relation to project tolerances agreed with corporate or programme management

- Review the Business Case to ensure that the project is still justified

- Review the key risks to ensure that the exposure is still acceptable and that response actions are planned

- Obtain decisions from outside the project for any potential deviations beyond project tolerances. For example, if this project is part of a programme, programme management will have to examine the likely impact on the programme and take appropriate action

- Authorize the Project Manager to proceed with the submitted plan (Stage Plan or Exception Plan) or instruct the Project Manager to prematurely close the project.

Communicate:

- Inform stakeholders (corporate or programme management and other interested parties) on project progress.

Give ad hoc direction

8

8 Give ad hoc direction

Purpose

Giving ad hoc direction is an important aspect of a Project Board member's role, providing opportunities to support the Project Manager, communicate and delegate effectively (consistent with the duties and behaviours listed in Chapter 3).

Project Board members can provide direction individually or collectively. The purpose of this activity is to ensure that there is a consistent and thorough mutual understanding between the Project Board, the Project Manager, Project Assurance and the external stakeholders throughout the project's life.

What to expect from the Project Manager

It is to be expected that on occasions the Project Manager will wish to clarify the interpretation of key aspects of the project (e.g. scope, quality requirements, the impact of external changes) with Project Board members (and vice versa).

The extent of giving ad hoc direction is a matter of judgement – an experienced Project Manager should not require continual direction or reassurance; but allowances should be made for less-experienced Project Managers or those unfamiliar with the particular type of project concerned.

8.1 CONTEXT

Project Board members may offer guidance or respond to requests for ad hoc direction at any time during the project (see Figure 8.1) –

Chapter 3 describes how this occurs during Starting up a Project.

Ad hoc direction may be given by the Project Board collectively or by individual members, i.e. within their specific spheres of responsibility.

There are a variety of circumstances that might prompt ad hoc interventions, including:

- Responding to requests (e.g. when options need clarifying or where areas of conflict need resolving)
- Responding to reports (e.g. Highlight Report, Exception Report, Issue Report)
- Responding to external influences (e.g. changes in corporate priorities)
- Project Board members' individual concerns.

In PRINCE2, the relationship between the Project Board and the Project Manager is centred on the plans. In giving ad hoc direction, Project Board members must always bear in mind what has been agreed in plans and what impact any direction they may give may have on the plans.

8.1.1 Consultations

8.1.1.1 Planning

Project Board members should be accessible to planners to provide supportive guidance during planning activity, particularly during project initiation. Each of the Project Board members will have their own focus of attention and their own sphere of expertise to bring to plans but, to fulfil their duty to provide unified direction, they must also ensure that the guidance offered by individual Project Board members is mutually consistent. This

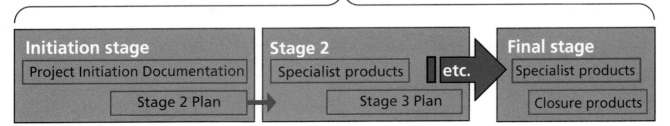

Figure 8.1 Give ad hoc direction

means that Project Board members may need to check with each other and ensure that they are providing direction consistently with each other and with approved plans (ad hoc direction, not 'knee-jerk' direction').

Once a plan has been established, Project Board members should adopt 'management by exception'. Needs for ad hoc direction may then arise in the course of the following activities:

8.1.1.2 Progress control

- If the Project Manager has trouble keeping the effort in line with the plan
- If resources are not available to do the work
- If the Project Manager needs clarification for an aspect of the plan
- If the Project Assurance function or a Project Board member raises a concern about progress in relation to the plan.

8.1.1.3 Quality control

- If the Project manager needs clarification over aspects of quality, e.g. the relative priorities of different expectations
- If the Project Manager encounters persistent shortcomings in the quality of products, e.g. from a particular third-party supplier
- If there is a complaint about quality from outside the project
- If the Project Assurance function or a Project Board member has a concern about product quality.

8.1.1.4 Change control

- If the Project Manager encounters a significant issue which may impact the plan
- If the Project Assurance function or a Project Board member raises a concern about whether some aspect of the plan is appropriate.

8.1.1.5 Risk management

- If the Project Manager identifies a significant new risk
- If the Project Assurance function or a Project Board member identifies a significant new risk
- If a combination of risks threatens the progress or viability of the project
- If the probability of a serious risk increases
- If a risk event actually occurs and planned countermeasures have to be implemented.

8.1.1.6 Benefits review

- If benefits are considered at risk – or additional potential benefits have been identified
- If changes are proposed to benefits measurements or the Benefits Review Plan.

8.1.1.7 Communication

- If there are any internal or external requests for more information
- If the Project Assurance function or a Project Board member is concerned about the wider awareness or perceptions of the project.

So direction may either be requested by the Project Manager or the Project Assurance function, or it may be volunteered by the Project Board member(s).

8.1.2 Project Board teamwork – unified direction

However the ad hoc direction is prompted, the individual Project Board member should consider:

- Whether they can confidently give the direction on the Project Board's behalf
- Whether the subject is really in another Project Board member's sphere of interest (and whether that member needs to be consulted first)
- Whether the direction needs to be cleared with the Project Board as a whole.

8.2 RESPOND TO REQUESTS

8.2.1 Types of request

The Project Board is likely to receive a number of requests for advice from the Project Manager, covering:

- A request for change
- An off-specification
- A problem or concern.

Formal requests will be raised in the form of an Issue Report. The composition for an Issue Report can be found in Appendix A – but it essentially documents the cause, impact, options and recommendation for dealing with the request.

8.2.2 Project Board decisions

Resource issues, in particular, frequently have to be escalated to Project Board members. Committing

Table 8.1 Responding to requests

Request	Project Board (or Change Authority) response	Considerations
Request for change	■ Approve the change ■ Reject the change ■ Defer decision ■ Request more information ■ Ask for an Exception Plan (if the request for change cannot be implemented within the limits delegated to the Change Authority).	If a request for change involves extra cost, there are three principal ways to fund it: ■ Use the change budget (if being used and if of sufficient size) ■ Increase the project budget ■ De-scope other elements of the project. Tolerance should not be used to fund requests for change.
Off-specification	■ Grant a concession ■ Reject the off-specification ■ Defer decision ■ Request more information ■ Ask for an Exception Plan (if the concession cannot be granted within the limits delegated to the Change Authority).	The Project Board may decide to accept the off-specification without corrective action. This is referred to as a concession. When a product is granted a concession, the Product Description will need to be revised before the product is handed over to the user.
Problem/concern	■ Provide guidance ■ Ask for an Exception Plan	Could the problem/concern be resolved by relaxing the stage tolerances?

resources is a key Project Board duty. The Project Manager should be expected to provide adequate notice of resource requirements and to negotiate the resourcing needs and timing in the course of planning.

However, if the agreed resources are not then made available according to plan, progress may be affected quickly and seriously. In these circumstances, the intervention of Project Board members inevitably carries more weight than the Project Manager's efforts.

8.2.3 Frequency of requests

Project Board members should be generally receptive to informal requests for direction. However, the nature and frequency of the requests can provide indications of strengths and weaknesses at the project management level.

Project Board members should expect frequent requests whenever plans are being prepared, but if requests continue to arise after the plan is approved, look for clues:

■ Is the Project Manager sufficiently experienced?
■ Is the plan sufficiently clear and detailed?
■ Are the requirements sufficiently stable?
■ Are the tolerances too tight?

Anything that may have a significant impact on the plan should be recorded as a risk, problem/concern, request for change or off-specification – is this happening? If so, are the issues really important or just trivia? If not, is the Project Manager maintaining adequate change control/Risk Management?

Are the Project Assurance arrangements adequate/appropriate? Should the Project Board delegate more or less authority to the Project Manager and/or to Project Assurance? Or should the manager set up a working level Change Authority?

Many issues do need to be escalated to the Project Board, e.g. any significant changes to scope, approach, products, budgets or schedules. If the requests are reasonable and there is evidence that the plans and project management disciplines are operating adequately, Project Board members can respond with appropriate guidance and help – and be reassured that the day-to-day management is secure.

However, if the clues point to project management weaknesses, Project Board members may need to drill down further – or direct Project Assurance efforts – to check on the adequacy of plans and the application of controls and to identify and resolve the weaknesses.

8.3 RESPOND TO REPORTS

8.3.1 Highlight Reports

During the delivery stages, the Project Board should 'manage by exception'. Members will be kept up-to-date by Highlight Reports from the Project Manager. These are designed to be concise, but they can contain as much information as the Project Board requires. Be aware that too frequent or too lengthy reports may well constrain a busy Project Manager's ability to lead and communicate.

Highlight Reports are intended for information only – to keep Project Board members in touch with progress and build confidence that the work is on track. Nevertheless, they will often prompt questions in the minds of Project Board members:

- There may be early indications of progress difficulties
- There may be outstanding or persistent issues
- There may be requests for change that are of interest – or a build up of simple changes
- There may be new risks.

Project Managers often complain about the time they have to spend on reporting, given the apparent lack of interest/response to the reports. Responding to Highlight Reports provides evidence of a Project Board member's interest in and commitment to the work – and their understanding of the framework of plans and controls. There may also be some simple opportunities for Project Board members to provide valuable assistance at the working level.

Highlight Reports are often also used to communicate progress outside the project management team, e.g. to stakeholders and interested line managers. This is an efficient way of avoiding the need for additional reports but it can encourage interventions or even direction from outside the project management team. When this occurs it needs to be managed sensitively, both by the Project Manager and Project Board members. The Project Manager should refer any suggested changes of approach or direction, or complaints about project progress, to the appropriate Project Board member (or to someone assigned a Project Assurance role).

Project Board members (and others with responsibilities in the project) should always make clear to other stakeholders how the project management team works and where accountabilities lie.

8.3.2 Exception Reports

In contrast to Highlight Reports, Exception Reports always require a response from Project Board members. They are alerts to the need for replanning. In all likelihood the Project Manager will have consulted Project Board members informally about the contents beforehand.

Exception Reports are evidence of good project management – irrespective of any failings that may have caused the exception – especially if the report is constructive, with good options for corrective action.

What Project Board members want to know from an Exception Report is:

- What is the nature of the exception?
- What is the impact of the exception on the products and plans?
- What would happen if the Project Manager just carried on with the stage?
- What options have been considered for resolving the exception? Why is the recommended option preferred?
- What is the potential impact on the Business Case?
- Was the exception anticipated as a project risk? What is the impact of the exception on project risks?
- What triggered the exception? Are there any significant lessons to be learned from the exception? Root causes? Corrective actions?

The Executive's concern is that the exception is managed properly. The Senior User will wish to know whether the exception resulted from user-related issues and, if so, how best to help resolve them and capture the lessons. Similarly, the Senior Supplier will be concerned to resolve any specialist technical issues and ensure that related lessons are identified, recorded and analysed. As always, Project Board members should make every effort to support the replanning exercise.

The Project Board can respond to an Exception Report in one of three ways:

- Adjust the tolerances, or use their influence to remove the cause of the exception, so that work can proceed based on the original Stage Plan

- Ask the Project Manager to prepare and submit an Exception Plan (see Chapter 7)
- In a situation where the Business Case is no longer viable, request that the project is prematurely closed (see Chapter 9).

If there is a series of manageable exceptions, the Project Board may need to reconsider the stage tolerances and provide the Project Manager with more discretion.

8.4 RESPOND TO EXTERNAL INFLUENCES

It is the particular responsibility of Project Board members to be sensitive to factors in the external project environment, which may have an impact on project viability or plans.

It demonstrates a good professional awareness of project disciplines to discuss external factors as potential issues and risks. Alerting the Project Manager to factors in the wider environment can often affect the project's Communication Management Strategy and may need to be reflected in the preparation of plans.

If external influences or events have a decisive impact on the Business Case, risks or plans, the other Project Board members should be alerted and the Project Manager informed so that the need to invoke the exception process can be considered.

8.4.1 Business, corporate or programme management influences

Part of the Executive's responsibility is to be aware of changes in corporate or programme strategies which affect the project, but it is possible that these may also come to light via other Project Board members. For instance, Senior Suppliers may become aware of new standards, methods, techniques or equipment that might have a bearing on the development of the solution; Senior Users may similarly learn of new requirements or market changes that are relevant.

All Project Board members should be alert to changes in the host environment which may impact the project.

For larger projects, it is important to recognize that the influences operate both ways. The project has needs and obligations which also have to be respected in the wider business environment. So

Example of beneficial external influence

In an IT services company, a manager was acting as Senior Supplier on the Project Board of several projects. In the course of one project he discovered that some expensive new equipment had been ordered which was subsequently found to be surplus to requirements. He was quickly able to redirect the equipment to a second project (with a different customer), offsetting the potential for wasted expenditure.

it is often part of the Project Board members' responsibilities to champion and advocate the project in the wider corporate and business environment (just as the director of a line function would do for their department). However, if the project is part of a programme, this wider business engagement would normally be managed, or at least coordinated, at programme level.

8.4.2 'PESTLE' influences

Depending on the scope of the project, similar considerations may apply to the wider project environment. PESTLE is a commonly used acronym for the types of influence that might be encountered in many projects and all sectors, i.e. Political, Economic, Social, Technological, Legislative and Environmental.

For instance, project Executives and Senior Users (particularly for government projects) are frequently aware of potential Budget or legislative proposals that may impact their projects or represent risks. Senior Suppliers, similarly, may be aware of technology changes relevant to the project that might merit a significant change in the project approach or the current proposed solution. It demonstrates a good professional awareness of project disciplines for Project Board members to discuss external factors.

Project Managers are often, of necessity, very focused on delivering in accordance with current plans. By contrast, Project Board members will have a wider perspective. It is not difficult to imagine the potential impact – both on project work and potential risks and opportunities – of major changes such as:

- The microcomputer revolution in the 1980s
- The internet in the 1990s
- The 'credit crunch' that emerged in 2008

- The expansion of the European Union
- Global warming
- Fluctuating oil prices
- Rising food prices
- Globalization
- Off-shore outsourcing.

Accordingly, it is easy to see that where Project Board members identify the potential impact of such changes early in the project, they can influence the results of the work immensely – whether by limiting the damage, reducing costs or significantly increasing benefits such as competitive advantage.

8.5 FOCUS OF INDIVIDUAL BOARD MEMBERS

8.5.1 The Executive's focus

- Internal or external factors affecting the project's Business Case
- Internal or external factors affecting the ability to realize the full scale of intended benefits – or opportunities to exploit additional benefits
- The effectiveness of the project's organization, plans and controls and the appropriate tailoring of PRINCE2 disciplines
- Contractual arrangements with suppliers, partners or consortia.

8.5.2 The Senior User's focus

- Factors affecting the arrangements for realizing the benefits during and after the project and the level of confidence that the benefits will be achieved
- The proper definition and communication of requirements; the ability of the products (the solution) to fulfil operational requirements; the adequacy of ongoing support arrangements for the solution; the timeliness of the solution in relation to user deadlines
- Conflicting resource requirements – maintaining business-as-usual operations
- Factors affecting the ability to meet user/customer obligations. Availability of suitably qualified user personnel to support planning and quality control
- Factors affecting the transition of project products into service – the requirements of service, support and maintenance functions.

8.5.3 The Senior Supplier's focus

- The viability of the specialist technical aspects of delivery plans (including related costs and timescales)
- The selection of appropriate technical methods, equipment, techniques, tools and standards
- The viability of the solution
- The availability of suitably qualified personnel for critical specialist tasks
- Factors affecting the transition of project products into service – the requirements of service, support and maintenance functions
- Availability of team resources. Conflicting resource requirements – development and service/maintenance demands on personnel
- Maintaining supplier business margins (where commercial contracts apply)
- Factors affecting the supply of sub-contracted or third-party work – contract, risk or resource issues.

8.6 COMMUNICATION

8.6.1 Outside the team

Larger projects, particularly, will have an agreed Communication Management Strategy and Project Board members usually have important roles to play in formulating and delivering consistent messages about the project's objectives and progress.

The Executive is concerned to keep corporate business and programme management informed and to manage expectations at that level.

The Senior Users are concerned to manage the expectations of personnel who may not be involved in the project but will be impacted by its outcome – also, perhaps, customers and clients (including the public?) who may have some contact with the project's products.

Often the Senior Suppliers' concerns will be keeping their own, separate corporate and programme management informed and managing supplier business expectations – indeed, monitoring the viability of the suppliers' own Business Cases. Whether or not they represent external organizations, the Senior Suppliers may wish to promote the work of the project – e.g. any successes or innovations – in a sales, marketing or perhaps just a professional career context.

Formulating messages for newsletters, presentations, press releases etc. – or actively communicating the messages at promotional events – may represent a significant proportion of Project Board members' ad hoc commitments.

8.6.2 Within the team

It is essential that Project Board members make themselves accessible to the Project Manager. An open-door policy is often a practical necessity, i.e. for sound decision making but, more than that, it is also a public demonstration that the Project Manager carries the delegated authority of the Project Board.

Similar considerations apply for contacts with personnel who have delegated Project Assurance responsibilities. However, the aim is to operate as a cohesive project management team: Project Assurance should be encouraged to support the Project Manager (who carries the accountability), to advise and inform rather than instruct or 'police'.

Project work typically entails more risk than other business activity. It can often be challenging and stressful. Project Board members who are seen to be involved, who demonstrate commitment to the project and provide a steady hand at the wheel can have an effect on overall team morale which is disproportionate to the time they have to commit.

8.7   GIVE AD HOC DIRECTION: SUMMARY

PRINCE2 requires that Project Board members undertake the following responsibilities, collectively and individually, for giving ad hoc direction.

Actions required for giving ad hoc direction

Respond to requests:

- Review the request. This could be informal or formal (in the form of an Issue Report)
- Make a decision – approve, reject, defer decision, request more information
- Provide guidance to the Project Manager.

Respond to reports:

- Review the latest Highlight Report to understand the status of the project
- Be satisfied, through dialogue with the Project Manager, that the stage is progressing according to plan
- Make decisions on Exception Reports – adjust tolerances or approve responses to the exception as appropriate.

Respond to external influences:

- Ensure that the project is kept informed of external events that may affect it
- Ensure that the project remains focused on the corporate or programme objectives set and remains justified in business terms
- Ensure that the Project Manager is notified of any changes in the corporate or programme environment that may impact on the project and that appropriate action is taken
- Where the project is part of a programme, if there is to be a change in the composition of the Project Board, the advice and approval of programme management should be sought.

Communicate:

- Advise the Project Manager of any change to Project Board personnel

- Keep stakeholders (corporate or programme management and other interested parties) informed about project progress, as defined by the Communication Management Strategy.

Authorize project closure

9

9 Authorize project closure

Purpose

Authorizing project closure is effectively the last project activity. Its purpose is to confirm that the project has been concluded in an orderly manner before the remaining project management team is disbanded.

The Project Board needs to be assured that the products of the project work have been securely handed over and accepted by the functions responsible for using and maintaining them, that the nature and responsibility of any follow-on action has been agreed, that measures are in place to realize the benefits from the project, and that the participating organizations exploit any lessons learned.

What to expect from the Project Manager

Before the Project Board confirms closure, the Project Manager must ensure that all the specialist activities and products of the final stage are complete, including those required for handover and acceptance.

The Project Manager should produce an End Project Report, detailing the resolution of any outstanding issues or follow-on actions and summarizing any lessons.

The Project Manager also updates the Benefits Review Plan with details of any benefits measured to date and with the arrangements and responsibilities for future benefits reviews – though this may be handled by programme management if the project is part of a programme.

It is important that there is an orderly closure even if a project is terminated prematurely.

9.1 CONTEXT

The final stage of a PRINCE2 project should include the activities (and products) required for an orderly project closure (see Figure 9.1). Sometimes organizations choose to mandate 'closure stages' after the specialist delivery work of the project is complete, but this is not a requirement of the method.

In fact, project closure can occur in two broad contexts:

- When all the products have been delivered and accepted
- When the project is terminated prematurely, for whatever reason.

Closing a project prematurely does not necessarily imply failure – and often represents good project management practice. The project may need to be terminated for any number of reasons:

- Change of corporate/programme strategy
- Changing corporate/programme priorities
- Changing market, social, regulatory or legislative environment
- Technology changes and innovations
- Change of corporate management.

As well as:

- Weakening Business Case
- Resources no longer available
- Escalating costs
- Delays and loss of momentum.

Whether the project has been successful or not, whether the reasons for closure are perceived as positive or negative, it is always good practice to implement an orderly closure.

There are three priorities to consider:

- The realization of operational benefits from the project. Normally this depends on organizational capabilities:
  - To operate and maintain the solution after the project has closed
  - To derive the resulting business benefits.
- The measurement and analysis of the project's performance – its strengths and weaknesses – in order to promote organizational learning and continual improvement
- The systematic decommissioning of the project – reassignment of personnel, equipment, accommodation; contractual formalities; promotional, sales and marketing collateral etc.

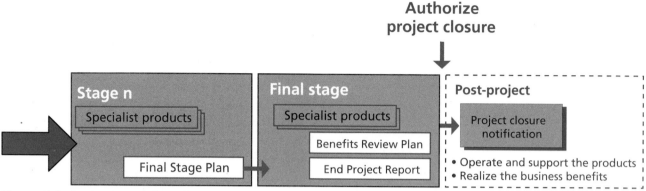

Figure 9.1 Authorize project closure

These three factors need to be provided for in the Stage Plan for the final stage (or, in the event of early termination, in the Exception Plan). The key products concerned are:

- The End Project Report
- Lessons Report
- Follow-on action recommendations
- The Benefits Review Plan.

The Project Board must ensure that these activities are covered when authorizing the relevant plans. (see Chapter 7).

Even a failed project may yield significant benefits – the Advanced Passenger Train (APT) example given in Chapter 7 illustrates this potential. It is always worthwhile to identify lessons that can be learned from project failures.

Note that the Project Board activity described in this chapter occurs after the closure work has been completed. Its purpose is for the Project Board to ensure that an orderly closure has been achieved – and, effectively, it constitutes the last act of the project.

9.2 CONFIRM HANDOVER AND ACCEPTANCE

There are normally at least two forms of handover and acceptance as outlined below.

9.2.1 Handover to users

The Project Board must confirm that all necessary user handover and acceptance activities and products have been completed and approved by the appropriate user authorities. This often includes user training.

The Senior User is accountable for the success of the project from this angle and, as such, they should have the responsibility in mind from the outset (project initiation).

This means understanding the related aspects of the Quality Management Strategy, such as user acceptance tests and certification, and ensuring that the right people are involved.

9.2.2 Handover to operational support

The Project Board must also confirm that all necessary operational, maintenance and support services (including any necessary contracts) are in place, and that handover and acceptance activities/products have been completed and approved by the appropriate service authorities.

The Senior User(s) and Senior Supplier(s) are both interested in this aspect of the project and should give this consideration at the outset (during initiation).

Handover to operational support means understanding the related aspects of the Quality Management Strategy (e.g. operational or service acceptance tests and certification, service level agreements, contracts, technical documentation and training) – and, again, ensuring that the right people are involved.

9.2.3 Concessions

Acceptance may be qualified by 'concessions', i.e. agreements to accept incomplete products or products with minor defects. A variety of other terms may be used on different project types – e.g. 'snag lists' or 'known errors'.

There are often good business reasons for accepting an imperfect solution, such as pressing legislative deadlines or opportunities for early benefits.

However, Project Board members must ensure that there are mutually satisfactory agreements on concessions and plans for their resolution, if required.

9.3 APPROVE THE END PROJECT REPORT

9.3.1 Measurement of project performance

The extent to which the performance of the project needs to be measured and analysed, and the degree of formality involved, depends on the value of the information to the participating organizations. This, in turn, depends on whether the organizations will be undertaking projects, especially similar projects, in the future. Whatever the motivation for measuring and analysing project performance, the measures have to be agreed at the outset, in project initiation and planning, or the information simply may not be collected.

Supplier organizations, in particular, will be concerned to use project metrics and lessons to refine their processes, methods, tools and estimation – promoting continual improvement.

In these circumstances, there are several metrics that may be valuable, for example:

9.3.1.1 Progress metrics

■ Effort (per key product?) compared with estimates
■ Costs (per key product?) compared with estimates
■ Elapsed time variances
■ Project management costs as a proportion of overall costs
■ Value of benefits to date (if any)
■ Revised estimates for future benefits.

9.3.1.2 Quality metrics

■ Defects (per key product and defect type?)
■ Defect penetration (comparing when the defect occurred with when it was discovered)
■ Quality control costs
■ Quality failure costs (reworks and off-specifications).

9.3.1.3 Change metrics

■ Number of requests for change (by technical phase?)
■ Costs of requests for change
■ Actual change costs in relation to approved change budgets, where applicable
■ Change effort/costs in relation to overall effort/costs
■ Issues that arose which may have been mitigated if they had been identified earlier as risks (e.g. avoidable issues).

9.3.1.4 Risk metrics

■ Occurrence of risks (by type)
■ Adequacy of risk budget
■ Percentage of actual risks that were on the original Risk Register.

Most if not all of these metrics can be derived from the project's Checkpoint Reports, Quality Register, Issue Register and Risk Register. Project Board members should ensure that metrics regarded as valuable for business purposes are retained for analysis by programme and/or corporate management.

A summary, at least, of the key performance measures should be included in the End Project Report.

9.3.2 Analysis of project performance

Depending on business needs, the End Project Report should include an analysis of the key metrics, including trends. This can be used for refining future estimates, root cause analysis of project-related problems and simply capturing lessons.

9.3.3 Lessons

Lessons can be learned from the measurement and analysis of project performance. But lessons can also be learned from anecdotal experience and recommendations by project management team members.

Though lessons should be identified and processed throughout the project, the key ones should also be recorded in the End Project Report. Moreover, Project Board members should ensure that the lessons are communicated effectively to programme and corporate management and to other stakeholders where appropriate. Ideally, this will be in a form that can be further analysed, alongside metrics and lessons from other projects (e.g. a database repository) – so that the business value is optimized.

End Project Reports are no less valuable for projects that are terminated prematurely – lessons learned from failure frequently have the most business value.

9.3.4 Follow-on action recommendations

In complex projects it is not unusual for there to be loose ends – outstanding risks or issues. Though these need to be managed properly, it is often uneconomical to have the project drag on until they are complete. In these circumstances, it makes sense to document and agree the issues and risks concerned, and to allocate them to user or operational support managers for further resolution.

Project Board members must ensure that these agreements are satisfactory and secure – and that they do not disguise any significant underlying problems.

The End Project Report should account for these arrangements and any other recommendations for follow-on actions.

9.3.5 Communicate the End Project Report

Lastly, once Project Board members are satisfied that the content is complete and accurate (both for their purposes and to meet programme and corporate business requirements) they should make sure that the information is communicated properly to all stakeholders. Consider getting an agreed summary of the project at project closure for use in promotional or reporting documents. This will save time in the future when Project Board members have dispersed.

When independent organizations are involved in the project, this often involves different versions of the report for different participants, with suppliers seeking to maximize the use of performance metrics and sales/marketing collateral.

The Communication Management Strategy may already cover the needs for communicating the End Project Report. The suggested format for the End Project Report, with generic quality criteria, is provided in the Product Description at Appendix A.

9.4 APPROVE THE BENEFITS REVIEW PLAN

The Benefits Review Plan agreed at project initiation outlines the overall approach to benefits management. Since it is often the case that most benefits will not be realized until after the project has closed, it needs to be updated and handed over to corporate or programme management to own.

The Project Board needs to check that the Benefits Review Plan includes activities to validate benefits and any customer quality expectations that cannot be measured until after the project's products have been in operational use for some time (for example reliability requirements).

> **Example of post-project benefits reviews**
>
> The UK Department of Health requires that benefits reviews for capital projects are held between 12 and 18 months after project closure.

Benefits Review Plans for projects that have been terminated prematurely should focus on safeguarding the latent benefits, e.g. intellectual property rights (IPR) and patents, from the project work already completed.

> **Example of a latent benefit**
>
> In the 1990s an international pharmaceutical company abandoned clinical trials for a product intended as a treatment for angina. The company discovered that patients using the drug had experienced some unforeseen clinical side effects, which provided a treatment for another unconnected medical condition. The company subsequently developed the drug to treat the other condition and it has since become a well-known market leader.

The suggested format for the Benefits Review Plan, with generic quality criteria, is provided in the Product Description at Appendix A.

9.5 COMMUNICATION

9.5.1 Issue the project closure notification

Issuing a project closure notification is the last act of the project – and the last Project Board duty.

The purpose of the notification is to advise those who have provided the support infrastructure and resources for the project that these can be withdrawn from a specific date – i.e. consistent with the Stage Plan activities for decommissioning the project and releasing resources.

The date should also act as the closing date for costs being charged to the project.

9.5.2 To the team

Successful projects are worth celebrating. Especially on medium- to large-scale projects, Project Board members should give some thought to marking completion with an appropriate gesture of gratitude before the teams disperse (NB: the nature of any gesture like this might require careful thought in case it could have unforeseen tax implications or be construed as an inappropriate reward.)

9.5.3 To the outside world

Successful projects are worth exploiting. Positive internal messages to programme and corporate management, success stories in press releases, and sales and marketing collateral should also be generated before the information loses value – or is simply lost. Ensure that key summaries are developed, tabled and approved during project closure while the Project Board members are still focused on this project.

9.6 SUGGESTED PROJECT BOARD AGENDA

A generic agenda for Project Board reviews was introduced in Chapter 3 (see section 3.6.1). The specific implementation suggested for confirming project closure is outlined in the boxed agenda.

Suggested agenda for authorizing project closure

1 Look back

Review the End Project Report

Review the Lessons Report and actions

2 Look forward

Review the Benefits Review Plan

Approve the follow-on action recommendations

3 Assess overall project viability

Confirm the final costs and expected benefits in the Business Case

4 Make a decision

Authorize project closure by approving a project closure notification.

9.7 AUTHORIZE PROJECT CLOSURE: SUMMARY

PRINCE2 requires that Project Board members undertake the following responsibilities collectively for authorizing project closure.

Actions required for authorizing project closure

Confirm handover and acceptance:

- Verify that the handover of the project product was in accordance with the Configuration Management Strategy and in particular that records of all required user acceptance and operational/maintenance acceptance exist
- Ensure that, where appropriate, the resulting changes in the business are supported and sustainable
- Ensure that any customer quality expectations that cannot be validated until after the project closes (e.g. performance levels regarding reliability) are included in the Benefits Review Plan as a post-project check.

Approve the End Project Report:

- The version of the Project Initiation Documentation which was approved at project initiation should be used as the baseline to assess how the project has deviated from its initial basis, and to provide information against which the success of the project can be judged
- Ensure follow-on action recommendations have been recorded correctly in the End Project Report and that the appropriate groups have been made aware of their responsibility for taking them forward
- Approve the End Project Report for distribution to stakeholders, for example corporate or programme management
- Review the Lessons Report and agree who should receive it. Ensure that the appropriate groups (for example corporate or programme management, or a centre of excellence) have been made aware of their responsibility for taking any recommendations forward.

Confirm the Business Case:

- Confirm the updated Business Case by comparing actual and forecast benefits, costs and risks against the Business Case approved with the Project Initiation Documentation (it may not be possible to validate all the benefits as some will not be realized until after the project is closed).

Approve the Benefits Review Plan:

- Review and gain approval for the updated Benefits Review Plan, ensuring that it addresses the expected benefits that cannot yet be validated
- As the Benefits Review Plan includes resources beyond the life of the project, responsibility for this plan needs to transfer to corporate or programme management.

Issue the project closure notification:

- Review and issue a project closure notification in accordance with the Communication Management Strategy
- Advise those who have provided the support infrastructure and resources for the project that these can now be withdrawn
- Release the resources provided to the project
- Provide a closing date for costs being charged to the project.

Reviewing benefits

10

10 Reviewing benefits

Purpose

A Benefits Review Plan is produced and approved, alongside the Business Case, during project initiation. Where benefits are achieved during a project, they are reviewed at stage boundaries, i.e. in the course of authorizing a Stage or Exception Plan and authorizing project closure. The Benefits Review Plan is updated and approval reaffirmed by the Project Board.

It is usually the case that the majority of the project's benefits will not be realized until after the project is closed. In such cases, the Benefits Review Plan will include activities to be performed post-project either by corporate or programme management. Those resources are not under the control of the Project Board. However, it is the responsibility of the Executive to ensure that the Benefits Review Plan includes any required post-project reviews and that corporate or programme management commits to undertaking them.

What to expect from the Project Manager

The Project Manager should prepare a Benefits Review Plan during project initiation. Then, during project delivery, the Project Manager implements the approved Benefits Review Plan. The plan is updated at stage boundaries to cover any benefits achievements, revised forecasts and/or changes approved by the Project Board. Performance in relation to the Benefits Review Plan is summarized in the End Stage Reports and then reviewed by the Project Board members when they authorize a Stage or Exception Plan.

Benefits achievements are also included in the End Project Report, at which point the Project Manager finalizes the post-project activity in the Benefits Review Plan for the Project Board's consideration when authorizing project closure. As the project is disbanding at this point, it is important that responsibilities for post-project benefits management are agreed and included in the plan.

10.1 CONTEXT

Project work is pointless unless the organization sponsoring the project perceives that it will contribute towards business benefits.

Where projects are part of a business change programme – and, in particular, when using OGC's Managing Successful Programmes (MSP) – the role of the projects is to 'create business outputs' (products). The role of the programme is to direct the projects in order to achieve longer-term outcomes (i.e. the results of the changes) and benefits (i.e. advantageous improvements) in line with the sponsoring organization's strategic objectives.

Thus the emphasis in PRINCE2 is on products and the emphasis in MSP is on outcomes and benefits. In an MSP programme, benefits management is normally undertaken at the programme level.

However, not all projects are organized to form part of a wider programme and not all programmes are structured in line with the MSP guidance. Moreover, it is often the case that some of the outcomes are achieved and benefits can be realized while the project is still in existence – and can therefore be managed within the scope of the project.

Regardless of whether the project exists within a programme or not, the senior managers who have governed a project are likely to have a role to play in ensuring that the organization gains the benefits expected from the investment.

10.2 HOLD BENEFITS REVIEWS

10.2.1 Prerequisites

For benefits realization to be effective, analysis needs to be undertaken and some decisions need to be made early in the project:

- Identify the benefits
- Select objective measures that reliably prove the benefits
- Collect the baseline measures (from which the improvements will be quantified)

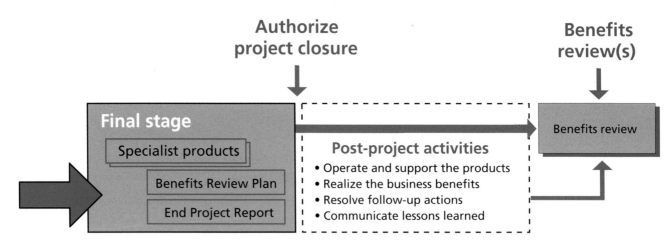

Figure 10.1 Post-project activities and benefits review

■ Decide how, when and by whom the benefit measures will be collected.

The arrangements for measuring benefits should be agreed when the Business Case is being developed in the Starting up a Project process and then updated at the end of each stage in the Managing a Stage Boundary process. Each benefit in the Business Case should be quantified (even if it is not possible to do so in cash terms), otherwise it is not possible to justify the investment in the first place. The measurement activity itself may well result in the inclusion of additional products in the Project Plan.

Some benefits may only be measured indirectly, in which case the Project Board should consider using other key performance indicators (KPIs) to extrapolate the benefits.

10.2.2 The reviews

The benefits reviews should be held as soon as it is practicable to demonstrate that the benefits have been realized or are capable of being realized. This should not be too soon – such that the measures are unreliable; nor too late for the findings to be useful. Also, later in the project, there may be continuity issues with key participants no longer being available after the project closes.

Consideration should be given to aligning the benefits reviews to the organization's strategic planning or budgeting cycles, as the extent to which benefits have been realized may influence the choice or priority of projects in the next planning cycle.

Example of measuring benefits directly

If one of the project benefits is a 10% reduction in customer complaints, then the project needs to consider:

■ Defining what constitutes a complaint
■ Ensuring there is a mechanism to count the complaints
■ Ensuring that there is baseline data to compare improvements
■ Defining the period over which the reduction will be compared (e.g. comparing the number of complaints in the same two-month period of successive years)
■ Whether the comparisons need to be adjusted for external factors (e.g. if the number of customers grows by 20%, then the number of complaints needs to be adjusted in some way to account for the different overall population).

Example of measuring benefits indirectly

Company X was able to prove the correlation between customer satisfaction and repeat orders and therefore initiated a set of projects to improve customer satisfaction for each aspect of the customer experience (marketing, sales, project delivery, product quality, support).

Where project delivery was concerned, 'being kept informed about project progress' was identified as a key factor in customer satisfaction. Consequently, a KPI was established for progress reporting – the 'average number of days since last progress update'. This became a predictive measure for increased customer satisfaction and, ultimately, repeat orders.

It is worth considering who leads the benefits reviews. PRINCE2 recommends that, as the custodian of the business interest, the Executive is accountable for benefits reviews but also recognizes that the Senior User is more directly responsible for achieving the business benefits. The rationale here is that the investment was made to achieve a beneficial outcome for users (often at their request): consequently, the Executive needs to verify that the return represents value for money for the business by asking the Senior User for evidence of the benefits gained. While this is valid in many project circumstances, it is not always the case, and project Executives should give careful consideration to responsibilities for benefits realization early on during project initiation.

10.3 CLOSE THE BUSINESS CASE

The Business Case for an investment normally survives the closure of the project. At the end of the project, it may be that only the project costs can be fully accounted for. Closing the Business Case at the end of a project does not provide a complete picture of the project's performance as, for example, the ongoing operational costs and benefits will almost certainly vary from those forecast.

Example of a benefits review after project closure

A project to implement an automated document storage and retrieval system was justified by two main benefits: a reduction in physical storage space requirements and a reduction in the number of temporary staff employed to store and retrieve information.

Twelve months after the project was completed, the benefits review demonstrated that the storage space had been reduced and the relevant leases terminated before they became due for renewal – and thus the expected cost savings on the estates were on track.

However, the organization still employed the same number of temporary staff. Managers had continued to use the 'temp budget' and simply switched staff from storage and retrieval work to other activities (without any associated business justification). The staff saving had not been realized.

Therefore as part of benefits review it is useful to monitor the running costs and benefits of the project's products for some time before closing the Business Case formally.

10.4 COMMUNICATION

The benefits reviews may highlight that:

- Some expected benefits were realized successfully
- Some expected benefits were not fully realized
- There were unplanned benefits (positive side effects)
- There were unplanned dis-benefits (negative side effects).

As the sole purpose of projects is to provide products that deliver benefits to the organization, then the benefits performance is possibly the most valuable aspect from which to learn lessons. The comparison of actual versus planned benefits and the root causes of any variations should be fed back into the corporate environment so that it can influence future investment decisions and project strategies.

10.5 SUGGESTED AGENDA FOR BENEFIT REVIEWS

Suggested benefits review agenda

1 Look back

Planned benefits accrued to date

Unplanned benefits accrued

Root cause(s) of variation

What lessons have been learned?

2 Look forward

Benefits forecast for the future

What are the likely lessons?

3 Assess Business Case performance

What are the current estimates for full-life costs?

How does the updated Business Case compare with the one agreed at project initiation?

4 Decision: close the Business Case

Is the investment sufficiently validated?

Do we need another benefits review?

A generic agenda for Project Board reviews was introduced in Chapter 3 (see section 3.6.1). However, as the Project Board no longer exists post-project, a suggested agenda for reviewing benefits is outlined in the boxed example.

10.6 REVIEWING BENEFITS: SUMMARY

PRINCE2 requires senior managers to undertake the following responsibilities when reviewing benefits.

Actions required for reviewing benefits

Hold the benefits review:

- Executive to decide when to hold the benefits review
- Senior User to prepare benefit statements for each benefit in the Business Case
- Identify root causes of variations between actual and forecast benefits
- Identify any lessons learned
- The Executive to decide whether the Business Case can be closed or whether further benefits reviews are required.

Close the Business Case:

- The Executive to update the Business Case with actual versus planned performance of the project with respect to full-life costs and accrued and forecast benefits.

Communicate:

- Pass on lessons learned to corporate or programme management.

Tailoring PRINCE2

11 Tailoring PRINCE2

Purpose

PRINCE2 is not a 'one-size fits all' method. An inherent characteristic of the method is that it should be tailored to suit the particular circumstances of each project – indeed, this is one of the seven fundamental principles of PRINCE2.

This chapter discusses the generic aspects that need to be considered and outlines a systematic approach for tailoring.

A closely related term is 'embedding', which addresses how PRINCE2 is best adopted, adapted and implemented in an organization or enterprise. Because the process of embedding focuses on the corporate organization – and not the individual projects – it is outside the scope of this manual.

A framework for embedding PRINCE2 is provided in the OGC's PRINCE2 Maturity Model (P2MM).

11.1 INTRODUCTION

Because the seventh principle of the method requires that it should be tailored to the project's environment, PRINCE2 cannot be applied properly without some consideration of tailoring.

In this chapter, tailoring is discussed in terms of:

- Factors in the external project environment that affect the application of PRINCE2
- Project-related factors that affect the application of PRINCE2
- How the application of PRINCE2 can be adapted in response to these various factors.

11.2 ENVIRONMENTAL FACTORS

11.2.1 Corporate maturity

Organizational maturity will have a large influence on the extent of the organizational support available when projects are set up. At high levels of maturity, there may be established arrangements such as:

- A **quality management system (QMS)** with corporate responsibilities (which must be recognized in the project arrangements), and standards and processes (which must be observed by the project). If the QMS includes processes for project management, then the assumption here is that they are already based on PRINCE2 and have been tailored to the needs of the organization, e.g. with templates and Product Descriptions for key management products.
- A **configuration management system** which the project must employ
- A **quality assurance** function which will contribute to the project's business and/or supplier assurance
- A **centre of excellence (CoE)** with subject matter expertise for project management and/or the specialist aspects of the project work
- **Programme/project office(s)** with subject matter experts for project work
- **Technology support** in the form of equipment (e.g. for automation) and/or software tools.

Thus it can be seen that, at high levels of maturity, Project Board members and Project Managers can expect to receive a great deal of corporate support and advice on the application of PRINCE2. A mature environment should also be flexible enough to accommodate changes, e.g. for a novel project that does not 'fit' well within the constraints of the current QMS, by allowing for 'concessions' (approved non-conformances) or process improvements.

At intermediate levels of maturity, some of these aspects of support may be present. At the lower levels of maturity, without these advantages, a tailored management framework for the project must be established, from scratch, during project initiation.

11.2.2 Project within a programme

If the project is part of a programme, some of the characteristics (above) of a mature organization are likely to be present (especially a programme office). Additionally:

- **Benefits management** (including benefits review planning) is likely to be conducted at programme level – especially in an MSP programme environment
- The **Starting up a Project** process is likely to be a programme-level process and, in effect, the project will start with Initiating a Project (based on a Project Brief approved at programme level) and the appointment of a project Executive
- **Risk, change and progress** themes at programme and project management levels will have to be carefully integrated so that impact assessment and escalation processes at the project level take into account the wider programme perspective.

11.2.3 Multi-organization

Projects involving multiple autonomous organizations, e.g. consortia, entail additional risk – in proportion to the number of organizations involved. This is mainly because each of the participating organizations has its own discrete business interest and objectives.

Representing the various interests in the project management team structure needs to be carefully thought out – by analysing the business, user and supplier relationships between the participants. In practice, each participating organization will usually implement some form of business assurance to review and safeguard its own business interests.

Another factor is that each organization may have its own QMS, so that agreement must be reached between the parties on which aspects of the various QMSs should be implemented in the joint project.

11.2.4 Commercial

Contractual relationships between customers and suppliers also need to be carefully analysed. Who will take the lead in the project? PRINCE2 generally assumes that the customer 'owns' the project – hence, that it is customer business and user representation that must feature in the project management team structure. However, this is not always the case nowadays. In many contracts the customers aim to safeguard their business interests and benefits in the contract terms, e.g. with payments to suppliers linked to the achievement of customer business benefits ('sharing the risk'). In this case, the customer often prefers that project

management is undertaken by the supplier, at arm's length. Consequently it is the supplier that often assumes the business interest (as well as the supplier interest) and the customer is represented by the user interest in the organization.

11.2.5 Business priority

As with scale and complexity, business priority (i.e. in relation to other projects in the organization) should have a bearing on the level of sophistication and formality in the project's plans and controls. Simple projects may implement PRINCE2 in a less formal manner, perhaps using bullet-point presentations and telephone conferences; whereas high-priority projects are more likely to require formal documentation and face-to-face meetings.

The experience and/or track record of the Project Manager may also be a factor here. Clearly it is preferable to put higher-priority projects in a safe pair of hands and allow junior Project Managers to learn their trade working on lower-priority work.

11.2.6 Standards

Even if the corporate or programme management does not have an established QMS, there may be discrete corporate standards for documentation control, specialist project lifecycle models, approvals, or other, similar disciplines. In addition, there are almost always industry, regulatory and/ or health and safety standards which must be observed.

The application of PRINCE2 must have due regard for these constraints.

11.2.7 Geography

The geographical disposition of the project management team(s) may have a bearing on the project management team structure and on the level of formality required in Project Plans and controls. If key project activities are dispersed across a number of centres, it may be worth considering whether a programme-type governance would be more suitable (other criteria for distinguishing programmes from projects are discussed in section 6.1.10). Generally, more formality is required where project management and personnel are physically remote from each other.

Even weather may be a factor. Undertaking work in a remote location and in wintry weather conditions is liable to be prone to additional delays – which should be reflected in planning and risk management.

11.2.8 Culture

Wherever possible, wider cultural norms should be recognized in tailoring. Many of these may relate to the project (matrix) organization, e.g. matching it to the local corporate hierarchies – which may be more strictly observed in Eastern countries than in the West.

'Management by Exception' can be difficult to implement in some management cultures where a more hands-on form of management is the norm. This can be accommodated by arranging additional confidence-building meetings for the Project Board during the stages. Provided that management stages and stage tolerances are implemented and observed, this is still consistent with the PRINCE2 principles.

11.2.9 Terminology

The terms used for PRINCE2 roles and documentation are unimportant as long as the meaning of the term is understood and implemented. It simply does not matter whether the Project Board is known as the 'Project Steering Group', the Project Initiation Documentation as the 'Project Charter', the checkpoint as a 'progress meeting' or the Highlight Report is a 'Progress Report'. What matters is that the terms in use accurately equate to their respective functions and composition in PRINCE2.

11.3 PROJECT-RELATED FACTORS

11.3.1 Scale

In general use, the term 'project' tends to have a very loose meaning and is applied to initiatives as widely different as the construction of the A380 Airbus or building a domestic garage. The fact that a project is relatively large-scale, alone, may not have much impact on the application of PRINCE2. Projects with complex interdependencies or high business priority are more likely to require higher levels of formal discipline.

Management should be careful not to over-burden simple projects with formality. Full-scale PRINCE2 implementations really only apply when the effort merits some form of Business Case and a temporary

organization of its own. Otherwise, smaller jobs can usually be managed effectively as free-standing Work Packages (or grouped with similar Work Packages and managed as a maintenance or support service).

11.3.2 Complex interdependencies

A project may be regarded as complex for many different reasons. For instance, there may be a single highly complex task in an otherwise simple project; or the project might be considered complex because of environmental factors considered in section 11.2. Complexity, here, refers to the nature and number of specialist interdependencies (between the products and activities) that have to be managed.

Complex interdependencies may apply in a single-discipline project – such as in engineering. These types of project require highly rigorous levels of planning and technical control – the technical controls being quality and change. In particular, sophisticated configuration management is likely to be necessary.

Another example of complexity may be a multi-discipline project, where different 'work-streams' employ markedly different specialist skills, e.g. implementing a new patient administration system (PAS) in the hospitals of a healthcare trust: this might involve software development, hardware and network infrastructure changes, re-engineering of the hospitals' business processes, training, changing the interfaces to General Practitioner systems etc. Again, rigorous technical controls and configuration management would be needed. In this case, it is worthwhile considering whether the project would be better managed as a programme, with the individual projects based on the different workstreams.

11.3.3 Team maturity

The maturity of the project management team may influence some of the control decisions. For example, shorter management stages might be implemented for a novice Project Manager, so that the Project Board can monitor progress more closely; whereas longer stages may be employed for a more experienced project management team.

11.3.4 Project type

A project's type is normally defined by its core specialist activity – engineering, construction, software, procurement etc. Many types of project have established, industry-recognized 'lifecycle models'. These models are extremely helpful for planners, predefining many of the specialist and quality activities required. For example, in software applications development there are currently two broad types of lifecycle model, known as 'waterfall' and 'agile'. As is the case in this example, different models, even in the same discipline, may have markedly different characteristics. Nevertheless, all lifecycle models can be expressed in terms of the products that must be created with their respective quality criteria and can therefore be integrated readily in a PRINCE2 management environment.

For a novel project, where there is no reliable lifecycle model available, the product-based planning technique supplied with PRINCE2 offers a reliable solution where planners have to start with a blank sheet of paper.

11.4 WHAT DOES TAILORING INVOLVE?

This section considers how each element may or may not be tailored and proposes a logical generic approach.

11.4.1 Principles

The PRINCE2 principles should always be applied. The manner in which they are applied may vary but, if any principle is removed, the project is no longer complying with PRINCE2. The value of the principles in tailoring is as a check – are we still applying all the principles?

11.4.2 Themes

Adapting a theme does not necessarily mean modifying the method. In most cases, the environmental and project factors are incorporated into the project's strategies and controls. Relevant corporate or programme policies and standards are captured and documented in the project's Risk Management Strategy, Quality Management Strategy, Configuration Management Strategy and Communication Management Strategy. These management products will describe the procedures to be used on the project that fulfil the requirements of the corporate or programme organization. The level of control required will influence the formality and frequency of reviewing and reporting.

11.4.3 Processes

All the PRINCE2 process activities need to be done; it is just that the responsibilities for performing the activities may change (if roles have been adapted) and references to the management products may need to change (if any management products have been adapted).

11.4.4 Environment

Tailoring the external environment of the project is more generally addressed in embedding, i.e. the process of implementing PRINCE2 across an organization, rather than for an individual project. Nevertheless, where there is large-scale project work, there may be some measures that can be taken in the host environment. For example:

- Finance/budget provisions: projects very often span organizations' financial years and may well be disrupted if they are conducted in the context of an annual budget cycle. Large projects are usually better considered as capital investments
- 'Recognition' of projects: organizations are typically managed as 'line structures' responsible for permanent functions, finance, procurement, production, customer services etc. Projects are temporary, cross-functional organizations – consequently they tend to receive less recognition in corporate processes and decision making. The more that projects and/or business change becomes important to corporate objectives, the more recognition should be accorded to the temporary programme and project structures. Some organizations are fully 'projectized', i.e. projects/programmes become the main context for decision making and line functions simply provide resources and administrative/quality services to the various categories of personnel engaged on project work.

With these considerations in mind, a logical approach to tailoring is illustrated in Figure 11.1.

11.5 ADAPTING THE THEMES

The following sections illustrate only a few of the ways the PRINCE2 themes can be tailored.

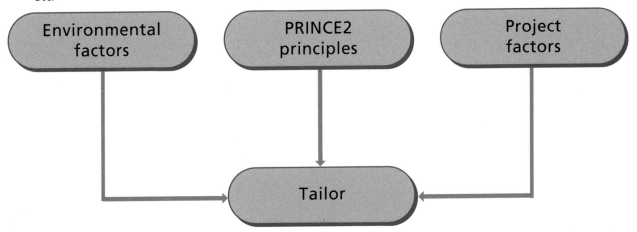

- Multi-organization
- External customer/supplier
- Corporate standards
- Within a programme
- Organization maturity
  (e.g. centre of excellence)
- Terms and language
- Geography
- Organization culture
- Project priority
- etc.

- Scale
- Solution complexity
- Team maturity
- Project type and lifecycle model
- etc.

Environmental factors

PRINCE2 principles

Project factors

Tailor

- Adapt the themes (through the strategies and controls)
- Revise terms and language
- Revise Product Descriptions for the management products
- Revise role descriptions
- Adjust processes to match the above
- Record in the Project Initiation Documentation

Figure 11.1 Influences on the tailoring requirement

11.5.1 Business Case

- If the project is a part of a programme, the Business Case theme may be managed at programme level
- A Business Case itself may be informal (some slides with bullet points) or formal (including a full-scale investment appraisal). The effort expended on the Business Case should be in proportion to the scale of the investment and risks involved
- Similar considerations apply to the Benefits Review Plan.

11.5.2 Organization

- The PRINCE2 project management team structure is extremely flexible
- The Project Board should have at least two members – if one person can represent all three

interests (business, user and specialist), the work can logically be managed as a line task and PRINCE2 is not required

- Where there are multiple important user or supplier interests, more than one Senior User and/or Senior Supplier may be appointed. The recommended maximum number of Project Board members, however, is five
- Where it is considered that all the user or supplier interests cannot be effectively represented on the Project Board, user and/or supplier advisory boards can be set up, chaired respectively by the Senior User and the Senior Supplier. The purpose of the advisory boards is to resolve a consistent approach to the project, which the Senior User/Supplier can subsequently represent at Project Board meetings. However, where there are multiple important interests

involved in a project, it may be a clue that the effort should really be managed as a programme

- The Project Manager cannot also be a Project Board member
- There can only be one Project Manager in a PRINCE2 Project. However, in a commercial context, it is often the case that Project Managers are appointed both for the customer and the supplier. These circumstances can usually be handled in one of two ways:
  - If the customer Project Manager acts as the PRINCE2 Project Manager, the supplier Project Manager assumes the PRINCE2 role of Team Manager
  - If the supplier Project Manager acts as the PRINCE2 Project Manager, the customer Project Manager assumes the PRINCE2 role of business and/or user assurance.
- Project Assurance must be independent of the Project Manager and Project Support
- In a simple project, the Project Manager can also act as the Team Manager and Project Support
- Project Support may be provided from a programme office or a shared project office.

11.5.3 Quality

- The Quality Management Strategy documents how the quality theme will be tailored for the project
- The Quality Management Strategy itself can be a concise, bullet point summary or based on a more formal template
- Product Descriptions are essential but the amount of information in them can be varied (from bullet points to more precise definitions)
- Quality inspections/reviews can be formal (structured meetings with detailed quality records) or informal (simple Daily Log entries)
- Again, the levels of formality required should be judged in relation to the investment and risk involved for the business.

11.5.4 Plans

- All the components of a PRINCE2 plan should be present in every plan (e.g. resources, assumptions, external dependencies, risks, controls etc.) but the level of formality can be varied

- The Project Board may prefer longer stages or shorter stages. Long stages entail a greater degree of delegation, fewer management overheads and they take up less of the Project Board members' time. Short stages provide the Project Board with more control but at the expense of additional stage planning and Project Board involvement
- Sophisticated software scheduling tools can be used in planning and communicating complex projects
- For simple projects, simple tables or spreadsheets, listing the products with expected completion dates can act as perfectly effective schedules.

11.5.5 Risks

- The Risk Management Strategy documents how the risk theme will be tailored for the project
- Here again, the formality and effort involved in risk management should be in direct proportion to the level of business investment and risk involved in the project
- It is not always necessary to operate detailed contingency calculations or implement risk tolerances
- When other PRINCE2 themes are tailored down, perhaps because of the urgency to meet a real project deadline, the associated risks (whether to quality or business benefits) should be recorded and monitored.

11.5.6 Change

- The Configuration Management Strategy is frequently tailored to the host configuration management system
- Configuration management may be relatively simple, with manual document and version control and a relatively simple manual change control process
- On more complex projects, configuration management often requires a sophisticated configuration management database (CMdb), with 'booking in and booking out' safeguards to prevent corruption due to simultaneous activity on multiple changes
- Where a CMdb is used, the process implemented for business-level change control (problems/concerns, requests for change and off-specifications) needs to be integrated

smoothly with the more detailed and rigorous configuration controls

■ Many commercial contracts contain change control schedules which detail the process for managing contract changes. Again, the project's business-level change controls (problems/concerns, requests for change, off-specifications) need to be tailored so that the contractual impact of changes is assessed and the contracted change control process is invoked when necessary

■ Different Change Authority approaches can be implemented to suit particular projects. The Project Manager can act as the Change Authority at working level (but all issues that involve Project Initiation Documentation baseline changes must be escalated to the Project Board). An alternative is for the Project Assurance role to act as the Change Authority. Change Authority can also be populated from outside the project management team, e.g. at programme level

■ Scope tolerances may be an important control, particularly when a 'time-boxed' approach is favoured (fixed timescale/variable scope – typical of an 'agile' or 'iterative' approach to computer applications development).

11.5.7 Progress

■ Tailoring for the progress controls is documented in the controls section of the plans

■ The frequency of Checkpoints (working-level progress reviews) can be varied. For example, in a time-critical accommodation move that has to be completed over a weekend, Checkpoints may be conducted every three hours, whereas for most projects the interval is typically weekly

■ The frequency of Highlight Reports can also be varied. The Project Board may request a Highlight Report at any time if circumstances suggest they need an update

■ Tolerances may be generous, e.g. for an experienced Project Manager and team who can confidently be left to get on with the work; or they can be tight – if the Project Board wants to monitor stage activity more closely

■ Project Board meetings may be formal, face-to-face reviews, scheduled months ahead to make sure members are all available; or they may be video- or telephone conferences. The important factor here is that the decisions are well informed from the three different perspectives (business, user and supplier) and, if possible, collective. If Project Board members do not meet for the purpose, the risk of ill-informed decisions increases.

Appendix A: Product Description outlines

Appendix A: Product Description outlines

This appendix contains Product Description outlines for PRINCE2's defined management products. These are not full Product Descriptions as defined by Product Description in section A.17, as some elements, such as quality method, will vary depending on the project's needs. Format examples are provided, but these are not exhaustive. The contents of a Product Description for a management product should be tailored to the requirements and environment of each project.

Note that the numbering system in this appendix reflects the system used in the main volume, *Managing Successful Projects with PRINCE2* (TSO, 2009). Certain management products and/or subsections may not be included in this publication, which explains why the numbered headings given here are not always sequential. Those management products **not** included are in square brackets in the list below.

There are three types of management product: baselines, records and reports.

Baseline management products are those that define aspects of the project and, once approved, are subject to change control. These are:

- A.1 Benefits Review Plan
- A.2 Business Case
- A.4 Communication Management Strategy
- A.6 Configuration Management Strategy
- A.16 Plan (covers Project, Stage and, optionally, Team Plans)
- A.17 Product Description
- A.19 Project Brief
- A.20 Project Initiation Documentation
- A.21 Project Product Description
- A.22 Quality Management Strategy
- A.24 Risk Management Strategy
- A.26 Work Package.

Records are dynamic management products that maintain information regarding project progress. These are:

- [A.5 Configuration Item Records]
- [A.7 Daily Log]
- [A.12 Issue Register]
- [A.14 Lessons Log]
- [A.23 Quality Register]
- [A.25 Risk Register].

Reports are management products providing a snapshot of the status of certain aspects of the project. These are:

- [A.3 Checkpoint Report]
- A.8 End Project Report
- A.9 End Stage Report
- A.10 Exception Report
- A.11 Highlight Report
- A.13 Issue Report
- A.15 Lessons Report
- [A.18 Product Status Account].

Although records and reports are not subject to change control, they are still subject to other aspects of configuration management, such as version control, safe storage, access rights etc.

Management products are not necessarily documents, they are information sets that are used by the PRINCE2 processes so that certain roles can take action and/or make decisions.

Most of the baseline products evolve during pre-project and initiation stage activities as shown in Figure A.1. The baseline products are then reviewed and (possibly) updated at the end of each stage. Management products nested within higher-level management products are illustrated in the composition of each management product by reference to their appendix heading (e.g. if a Lessons Report is nested in another report, there will be a cross-reference to section A.15).

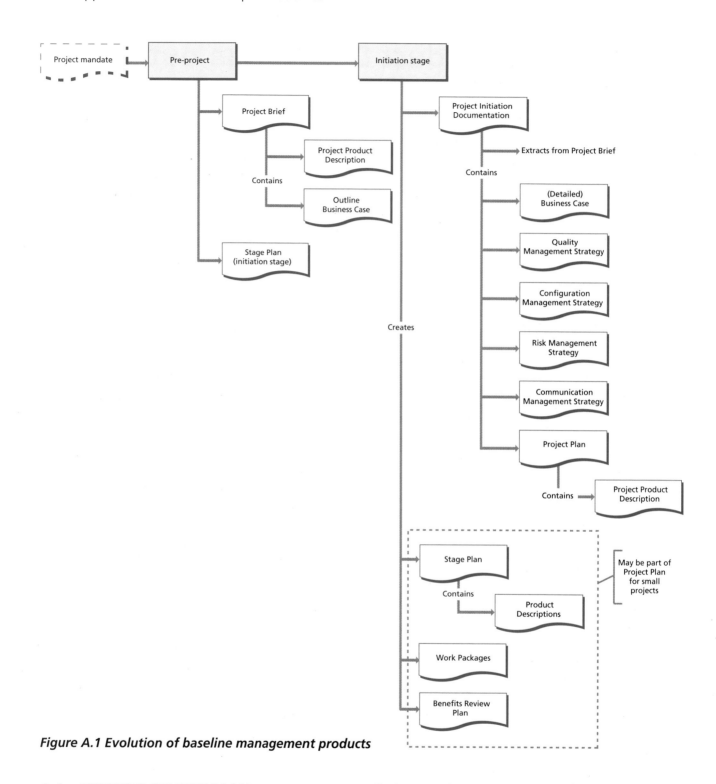

Figure A.1 Evolution of baseline management products

A.1 BENEFITS REVIEW PLAN

A.1.1 Purpose

A Benefits Review Plan is used to define how and when a measurement of the achievement of the project's benefits, expected by the Senior User, can be made. The plan is presented to the Executive during the Initiating a Project process, updated at each stage boundary, and used during the

Closing a Project process to define any post-project benefits reviews that are required.

The plan has to cover the activities to find out whether the expected benefits of the products have been realized and how the products have performed when in operational use. Each expected benefit has to be assessed for the level of its achievement and whether any additional time is needed to assess the residual benefits. Use of the project's products may have brought unexpected side-effects, either beneficial or adverse. Time and effort have to be allowed to identify and analyse why these side-effects were not foreseen.

If the project is part of a programme, the Benefits Review Plan may be contained within the programme's benefits realization plan and executed at the programme level. Post-project, the Benefits Review Plan is maintained and executed by corporate or programme management.

A.1.2 Composition

- The scope of the Benefits Review Plan covering what benefits are to be measured
- Who is accountable for the expected benefits
- How to measure achievement of expected benefits, and when they can be measured
- What resources are needed to carry out the review work
- Baseline measures from which the improvements will be calculated
- How the performance of the project's product will be reviewed.

A.1.4 Format and presentation

A Benefits Review Plan can take a number of formats, including:

- Document, spreadsheet or presentation slides
- Entry in a project management tool.

A.1.5 Quality criteria

- Covers all benefits mentioned in the Business Case
- The benefits are measurable and baseline measures have been recorded
- Describes suitable timing for measurement of the benefits, together with reasons for the timing
- Identifies the skills or individuals who will be needed to carry out the measurements
- The effort and cost to undertake the benefits reviews is realistic when compared with the value of the anticipated benefits
- Consideration is given to whether dis-benefits should be measured and reviewed.

A.2 BUSINESS CASE

A.2.1 Purpose

A Business Case is used to document the justification for the undertaking of a project, based on the estimated costs (of development, implementation and incremental ongoing operations and maintenance costs) against the anticipated benefits to be gained and offset by any associated risks.

The outline Business Case is developed in the Starting up a Project process and refined by the Initiating a Project process. The Directing a Project process covers the approval and re-affirmation of the Business Case.

The Business Case is used by the Controlling a Stage process when assessing impacts of issues and risks. It is reviewed and updated at the end of each management stage by the Managing a Stage Boundary process, and at the end of the project by the Closing a Project process.

A.2.2 Composition

- **Executive summary** Highlights the key points in the Business Case, which should include important benefits and the return on investment (ROI)
- **Reasons** Defines the reasons for undertaking the project and explains how the project will enable the achievement of corporate strategies and objectives
- **Business options** Analysis and reasoned recommendation for the base business options of: do nothing, do the minimal or do something
- **Expected benefits** The benefits that the project will deliver expressed in measurable terms against the situation as it exists prior to the project. Benefits should be both qualitative and quantitative. They should be aligned to corporate or programme benefits. Tolerances should be set for each benefit and for the aggregated benefit. Any benefits realization requirements should be stated
- **Expected dis-benefits** Outcomes perceived as negative by one or more stakeholders. Dis-benefits are actual consequences of an activity whereas, by definition, a risk has some uncertainty about whether it will materialize. For example, a decision to merge two elements of an organization onto a new site may have

benefits (e.g. better joint working), costs (e.g. expanding one of the two sites) and dis-benefits (e.g. drop in productivity during the merger). Dis-benefits need to be valued and incorporated into the investment appraisal

■ **Timescale** Over which the project will run (summary of the Project Plan) and the period over which the benefits will be realized. This information is subsequently used to help timing decisions when planning (Project Plan, Stage Plan and Benefits Review Plan)

■ **Costs** A summary of the project costs (taken from the Project Plan), the ongoing operations and maintenance costs and their funding arrangements

■ **Investment appraisal** Compares the aggregated benefits and dis-benefits to the project costs (extracted from the Project Plan) and ongoing incremental operations and maintenance costs. The analysis may use techniques such as cash flow statement, ROI, net present value, internal rate of return and payback period. The objective is to be able to define the value of a project as an investment. The investment appraisal should address how the project will be funded

■ **Major risks** Gives a summary of the key risks associated with the project together with the likely impact and plans should they occur.

A.2.4 Format and presentation

A Business Case can take a number of formats, including:

■ Document, spreadsheet or presentation slides
■ Entry in a project management tool.

A.2.5 Quality criteria

■ The reasons for the project must be consistent with the corporate or programme strategy
■ The Project Plan and Business Case must be aligned
■ The benefits should be clearly identified and justified
■ It should be clear how the benefits will be realized
■ It should be clear what will define a successful outcome
■ It should be clear what the preferred business option is, and why

■ Where external procurement is required, it should be clear what the preferred sourcing option is, and why
■ It should be clear how any necessary funding will be obtained
■ The Business Case includes non-financial, as well as financial, criteria
■ The Business Case includes operations and maintenance costs and risks, as well as project costs and risks
■ The Business Case conforms to organizational accounting standards (e.g. break-even analysis and cash flow conventions)
■ The major risks faced by the project are explicitly stated, together with any proposed responses.

A.4 COMMUNICATION MANAGEMENT STRATEGY

A.4.1 Purpose

A Communication Management Strategy contains a description of the means and frequency of communication to parties both internal and external to the project. It facilitates engagement with stakeholders through the establishment of a controlled and bi-directional flow of information.

A.4.2 Composition

■ **Introduction** States the purpose, objectives and scope, and identifies who is responsible for the strategy
■ **Communication procedure** A description of (or reference to) any communication methods to be used. Any variance from corporate or programme management standards should be highlighted, together with a justification for the variance
■ **Tools and techniques** Refers to any communication tools to be used, and any preference for techniques that may be used, for each step in the communication process
■ **Records** Definition of what communication records will be required and where they will be stored (for example, logging of external correspondence)
■ **Reporting** Describes any reports on the communication process that are to be produced, including their purpose, timing and recipients (for example, performance indicators)

- **Timing of communication activities** States when formal communication activities are to be undertaken (for example, at the end of a stage) including performance audits of the communication methods
- **Roles and responsibilities** Describes who will be responsible for what aspects of the communication process, including any corporate or programme management roles involved with communication
- **Stakeholder analysis**:
  - Identification of the interested party (which may include accounts staff, user forum, internal audit, corporate or programme quality assurance, competitors etc.)
  - Current relationship
  - Desired relationship
  - Interfaces
  - Key messages
- **Information needs for each interested party**:
  - Information required to be provided from the project
  - Information required to be provided to the project
  - Information provider and recipient
  - Frequency of communication
  - Means of communication
  - Format of the communication.

A.4.4 Format and presentation

A Communication Management Strategy can take a number of formats, including:

- Stand-alone product or a section of the Project Initiation Documentation
- Document, spreadsheet or mindmap
- Entry in a project management tool.

A.4.5 Quality criteria

- All stakeholders have been identified and consulted for their communication requirements
- There is agreement from all stakeholders about the content, frequency and method of communication
- A common standard for communication has been considered
- The time, effort and resources required to carry out the identified communications have been allowed for in Stage Plans

- The formality and frequency of communication is reasonable for the project's importance and complexity
- For projects that are part of a programme, the lines of communication, and the reporting structure between the project and programme, have been made clear in the Communication Management Strategy
- The Communication Management Strategy incorporates corporate communications facilities where appropriate (e.g. using the marketing communications department for distributing project bulletins).

A.6 CONFIGURATION MANAGEMENT STRATEGY

A.6.1 Purpose

A Configuration Management Strategy is used to identify how, and by whom, the project's products will be controlled and protected.

It answers the questions:

- How and where the project's products will be stored
- What storage and retrieval security will be put in place
- How the products and the various versions and variants of these will be identified
- How changes to products will be controlled
- Where responsibility for configuration management will lie.

A.6.2 Composition

- **Introduction** States the purpose, objectives and scope, and identifies who is responsible for the strategy
- **Configuration management procedure** A description of (or reference to) the configuration management procedure to be used. Any variance from corporate or programme management standards should be highlighted, together with a justification for the variance. The procedure should cover activities such as planning, identification, control (including storage/retrieval, product security, handover procedures etc.), status accounting, and verification and audit.
- **Issue and change control procedure** A description (or reference to) the issue and

change control procedures to be used. Any variance from corporate or programme management standards should be highlighted, together with a justification for the variance. The procedure should cover activities such as capturing, examining, proposing, deciding and implementing.

- **Tools and techniques** Refers to any configuration management systems or tools to be used and any preference for techniques that may be used for each step in the configuration management procedure

- **Records** Definition of the composition and format of the Issue Register and Configuration Item Records

- **Reporting** Describes the composition and format of the reports that are to be produced (Issue Report, Product Status Account), their purpose, timing and chosen recipients. This should include reviewing the performance of the procedures

- **Timing of configuration management and issue and change control activities** States when formal activities are to be undertaken, for example configuration audits

- **Roles and responsibilities** Describes who will be responsible for what aspects of the procedures, including any corporate or programme management roles involved with the configuration management of the project's products. Describes whether a Change Authority and/or change budget will be established.

- **Scales for priority and severity** For prioritizing requests for change and off-specifications and for determining the level of management that can make decisions on severity of issue.

A.6.4 Format and presentation

A Configuration Management Strategy can take a number of formats, including:

- Stand-alone document or a section of the Project Initiation Documentation
- Entry in a project management tool.

A.6.5 Quality criteria

- Responsibilities are clear and understood by both user and supplier
- The key identifier for the project's product(s) is defined

- The method and circumstances of version control are clear
- The strategy provides the Project Manager with all the product information required
- The corporate or programme strategy for configuration management has been considered
- The retrieval system will produce all required information in an accurate, timely and usable manner
- The project files provide the information necessary for any audit requirements
- The project files provide the historical records required to support any lessons
- The chosen Configuration Management Strategy is appropriate for the size and nature of the project
- Resources are in place to administer the chosen method of configuration management
- The requirements of the operational group (or similar group to whom the project's product will be transitioned) should be considered.

A.8 END PROJECT REPORT

A.8.1 Purpose

An End Project Report is used during project closure to review how the project performed against the version of the Project Initiation Documentation used to authorize it. It also allows the:

- Passing on of any lessons that can be usefully applied to other projects
- Passing on of details of unfinished work, ongoing risks or potential product modifications to the group charged with future support of the project's products in their operational life.

A.8.2 Composition

- **Project Manager's report** Summarizing the project's performance
- **Review of the Business Case** Summarizing the validity of the project's Business Case:
  - Benefits achieved to date
  - Residual benefits expected (post-project)
  - Expected net benefits
  - Deviations from the approved Business Case

- **Review of project objectives** Review of how the project performed against its planned targets and tolerances for time, cost, quality, scope, benefits and risk. Review the effectiveness of the project's strategies and controls
- **Review of team performance** In particular, providing recognition for good performance
- **Review of products**:
  - **Quality records** Listing the quality activities planned and completed
  - **Approval records** Listing the products and their requisite approvals
  - **Off-specifications** Listing any missing products or products that do not meet the original requirements, and confirmation of any concessions granted
  - **Project product handover** Confirmation (in the form of acceptance records) by the customer that operations and maintenance functions are ready to receive the project's product
  - **Summary of follow-on action recommendations** Request for Project Board advice about who should receive each recommended action. The recommended actions are related to unfinished work, ongoing issues and risks, and any other activities needed to take the products to the next phase of their life
- **Lessons Report** (see section A.15) A review of what went well, what went badly, and any recommendations for corporate or programme management consideration (and if the project was prematurely closed, then the reasons should be explained).

A.8.4 Format and presentation

An End Project Report can take a number of formats, including:

- Presentation to the Project Board (physical meeting or conference call)
- Document or email issued to the Project Board
- Entry in a project management tool.

A.8.5 Quality criteria

- Any abnormal situations are described, together with their impact
- At the end of the project, all issues should either be closed or become the subject of a follow-on action recommendation

- Any available useful documentation or evidence should accompany the follow-on action recommendation(s)
- Any appointed Project Assurance roles should agree with the report.

A.9 END STAGE REPORT

A.9.1 Purpose

An End Stage Report is used to give a summary of progress to date, the overall project situation, and sufficient information to ask for a Project Board decision on what to do next with the project.

The Project Board uses the information in the End Stage Report in tandem with the next Stage Plan to decide what action to take with the project: for example, authorize the next stage, amend the project scope, or stop the project.

A.9.2 Composition

- **Project Manager's report** Summarizing the stage performance
- **Review of the Business Case** Summarizing the validity of the project's Business Case:
  - Benefits achieved to date
  - Residual benefits expected (remaining stages and post-project)
  - Expected net benefits
  - Deviations from approved Business Case
  - Aggregated risk exposure
- **Review of project objectives** Review of how the project has performed to date against its planned targets and tolerances for time, cost, quality, scope, benefits and risk. Review the effectiveness of the project's strategies and controls
- **Review of stage objectives** Review of how the specific stage performed against its planned targets and tolerances for time, cost, quality, scope, benefits and risk
- **Review of team performance** In particular, providing recognition for good performance
- **Review of products**:
  - **Quality records** Listing the quality activities planned and completed in the stage
  - **Approval records** Listing the products planned for completion in the stage and their requisite approvals

- **Off-specifications** Listing any missing products or products that do not meet the original requirements, and confirmation of any concessions granted
- **Phased handover (if applicable)** Confirmation by the customer that operations and maintenance functions are ready to receive the release
- **Summary of follow-on action recommendations (if applicable)** Request for Project Board advice for who should receive each recommended action. The recommended actions are related to unfinished work, ongoing issues and risks, and any other activities needed to take the products handed over to the next phase of their life

- **Lessons Report** (if appropriate) (see section A.15) A review of what went well, what went badly, and any recommendations for corporate or programme management consideration
- **Issues and risks** Summary of the current set of issues and risks affecting the project
- **Forecast** The Project Manager's forecast for the project and next stage against planned targets and tolerances for time, cost, quality, scope, benefits and risk.

Where the End Stage Report is being produced at the end of the initiation stage, not all of the above content may be appropriate or necessary.

A.9.4 Format and presentation

An End Stage Report can take a number of formats, including:

- Presentation to the Project Board (physical meeting or conference call)
- Document or email issued to the Project Board
- Entry in a project management tool.

A.9.5 Quality criteria

- The report clearly shows stage performance against the plan
- Any abnormal situations are described, together with their impact
- Any appointed Project Assurance roles agree with the report.

A.10   EXCEPTION REPORT

A.10.1 Purpose

An Exception Report is produced when a Stage Plan or Project Plan is forecast to exceed tolerance levels set. It is prepared by the Project Manager in order to inform the Project Board of the situation, and to offer options and recommendations for the way to proceed.

A.10.2 Composition

- **Exception title** An overview of the exception being reported
- **Cause of the exception** A description of the cause of a deviation from the current plan
- **Consequences of the deviation** What the implications are if the deviation is not addressed for:
  - The project
  - Corporate or programme management
- **Options** What are the options that are available to address the deviation and what would the effect of each option be on the Business Case, risks and tolerances
- **Recommendation** Of the available options, what is the recommendation, and why?
- **Lessons** What can be learned from the exception, on this project or future projects.

A.10.4 Format and presentation

An Exception Report can take a number of formats, including:

- Issue raised at a minuted progress review (physical meeting or conference call)
- Document or email issued to the next-higher level of management
- Entry in a project management tool.

For urgent exceptions, it is recommended that the Exception Report is oral in the first instance, and then followed-up in the agreed format.

A.10.5 Quality criteria

- The current plan must accurately show the status of time and cost performance
- The reason(s) for the deviation must be stated, the exception clearly analysed, and any impacts assessed and fully described

- Implications for the Business Case have been considered and the impact on the overall Project Plan has been calculated
- Options are analysed (including any risks associated with them) and recommendations are made for the most appropriate way to proceed
- The Exception Report is given in a timely and appropriate manner.

A.11 HIGHLIGHT REPORT

A.11.1 Purpose

A Highlight Report is used to provide the Project Board (and possibly other stakeholders) with a summary of the stage status at intervals defined by them. The Project Board uses the report to monitor stage and project progress. The Project Manager also uses it to advise the Project Board of any potential problems or areas where the Project Board could help.

A.11.2 Composition

- **Date** The date of the report
- **Period** The reporting period covered by the Highlight Report
- **Status summary** An overview of the status of the stage at this time
- **This reporting period**:
  - Work Packages – pending authorization, in execution, and completed in the period (if the Work Packages are being performed by external suppliers, this information may be accompanied by purchase order and invoicing data)
  - Products completed in the period
  - Products planned but not started or completed in the period (providing an early warning indicator or potential breach of time tolerance)
  - Corrective actions taken during the period
- **Next reporting period**:
  - Work Packages – to be authorized, in execution, and to be completed during the next period (if the Work Packages are being performed by external suppliers, this information may be accompanied by purchase order and invoicing data)
  - Products to be completed in the next period

- Corrective actions to be completed during the next period
- **Project and stage tolerance status** How execution of the project and stage are performing against their tolerances (e.g. cost/ time actuals and forecast)
- **Requests for change** Raised, approved/rejected and pending
- **Key issues and risks** Summary of actual or potential problems and risks
- **Lessons Report** (if appropriate) (see section A.15) A review of what went well, what went badly, and any recommendations for corporate or programme management consideration.

A.11.4 Format and presentation

A Highlight Report can take a number of formats, including:

- Presentation to the Project Board (physical meeting or conference call)
- Document or email issued to the Project Board
- Entry in a project management tool.

A.11.5 Quality criteria

- The level and frequency of progress reporting required by the Project Board is right for the stage and/or project
- The Project Manager provides the Highlight Report at the frequency, and with the content, required by the Project Board
- The information is timely, useful, accurate and objective
- The report highlights any potential problem areas.

A.13 ISSUE REPORT

A.13.1 Purpose

An Issue Report is a report containing the description, impact assessment and recommendations for a request for change, off-specification or a problem/concern. It is only created for those issues that need to be handled formally.

The report is initially created when capturing the issue, and updated both after the issue has been examined and when proposals are identified for issue resolution. The Issue Report is later amended further in order to record what option was decided upon, and finally updated when the implementation has been verified and the issue is closed.

A.13.2 Composition

- **Issue identifier** As shown in the Issue Register (provides a unique reference for every Issue Report)
- **Issue type** Defines the type of issue being recorded, namely:
  - Request for change
  - Off-specification
  - Problem/concern
- **Date raised** The date on which the issue was originally raised
- **Raised by** The name of the individual or team who raised the issue
- **Issue Report author** The name of the individual or team who created the Issue Report
- **Issue description** A statement describing the issue in terms of its cause and impact
- **Impact analysis** A detailed analysis of the likely impact of the issue. This may include, for example, a list of products impacted
- **Recommendation** A description of what the Project Manager believes should be done to resolve the issue (and why)
- **Priority** This should be given in terms of the project's chosen scale. It should be re-evaluated after impact analysis
- **Severity** This should be given in terms of the project's chosen scale. Severity will indicate what level of management is required to make a decision on the issue
- **Decision** The decision made (accept, reject, defer or grant concession)
- **Approved by** A record of who made the decision
- **Decision date** The date of the decision
- **Closure date** The date that the issue was closed.

A.13.4 Format and presentation

An Issue Report can take a number of formats, including:

- Document, spreadsheet or database
- Entry in a project management tool

Not all entries in the Issue Register will need a separately documented Issue Report.

A.13.5 Quality criteria

- The issue stated is clear and unambiguous
- A detailed impact analysis has occurred
- All implications have been considered
- The issue has been examined for its effect on the tolerances
- The issue has been correctly registered on the Issue Register
- Decisions are accurately and unambiguously described.

A.15 LESSONS REPORT

A.15.1 Purpose

The Lessons Report is used to pass on any lessons that can be usefully applied to other projects.

The purpose of the report is to provoke action so that the positive lessons become embedded in the organization's way of working, and that the organization is able to avoid any negative lessons on future projects.

A Lessons Report can be created at any time in a project and should not necessarily wait to the end. Typically it should be included as part of the End Stage Report and End Project Report. It may be appropriate (and necessary) for there to be several Lessons Reports specific to the particular organization (e.g. user, supplier, corporate or programme).

The data in the report should be used by the corporate group that is responsible for the quality management system, in order to refine, change and improve the standards. Statistics on how much effort was needed for products can help improve future estimating.

A.15.2 Composition

- Executive summary
- Scope of the report (e.g. stage or project)
- A review of what went well, what went badly and any recommendations for corporate or programme management consideration. In particular:
  - Project management method (including the tailoring of PRINCE2)
  - Any specialist methods used

- Project strategies (risk management, quality management, communications management and configuration management)
- Project controls (and the effectiveness of any tailoring)
- Abnormal events causing deviations
- A review of useful measurements such as:
  - How much effort was required to create the products
  - How effective was the Quality Management Strategy in designing, developing and delivering fit-for-purpose products (for example, how many errors were found after products had passed quality inspections?)
  - Statistics on issues and risks
- For significant lessons it may be useful to provide additional details on:
  - Event
  - Effect (e.g. positive/negative financial impact)
  - Causes/trigger
  - Whether there were any early-warning indicators
  - Recommendations
  - Whether the triggered event was previously identified as a risk (threat or opportunity).

A.15.4 Format and presentation

A Lessons Report can take a number of formats, including:

- Oral report to the Project Board (could be in person or over the phone)
- Presentation at a progress review (physical meeting or conference call)
- Document or email issued to the Project Board
- Entry in a project management tool.

A.15.5 Quality criteria

- Every management control has been examined
- Statistics of estimates versus actuals are provided
- Statistics of the success of quality controls used are included
- Any appointed Project Assurance roles agree with the report
- Unexpected risks are reviewed to determine whether they could have been anticipated
- Recommended actions are provided for each lesson (note that lessons are not 'learned' until action is taken).

A.16 PLAN

A.16.1 Purpose

A plan provides a statement of how and when objectives are to be achieved, by showing the major products, activities and resources required for the scope of the plan. In PRINCE2, there are three levels of plan: project, stage and team. Team Plans are optional and may not need to follow the same composition as a Project Plan or Stage Plan.

An Exception Plan is created at the same level as the plan that it is replacing.

A Project Plan provides the Business Case with planned costs, and it identifies the management stages and other major control points. It is used by the Project Board as a baseline against which to monitor project progress.

Stage Plans cover the products, resources, activities and controls specific to the stage and are used as a baseline against which to monitor stage progress.

Team Plans (if used) could comprise just a schedule appended to the Work Package(s) assigned to the Team Manager.

A plan should cover not just the activities to create products but also the activities to manage product creation – including activities for assurance, quality management, risk management, configuration management, communication and any other project controls required.

A.16.2 Composition

- **Plan description** Covering a brief description of what the plan encompasses (i.e. project, stage, team, exception) and the planning approach
- **Plan prerequisites** Containing any fundamental aspects that must be in place, and remain in place, for the plan to succeed
- **External dependencies** That may influence the plan
- **Planning assumptions** Upon which the plan is based
- **Lessons incorporated** Details of relevant lessons from previous similar projects, which have been reviewed and accommodated within this plan
- **Monitoring and control** Details of how the plan will be monitored and controlled
- **Budgets** Covering time and cost, including provisions for risks and changes

- **Tolerances** Time, cost and scope tolerances for the level of plan (which may also include more specific stage- or team-level risk tolerances)
- **Product Descriptions** (see section A.17) Covering the products within the scope of the plan (for the Project Plan this will include the project's product; for the Stage Plan this will be the stage products; and for a Team Plan this should be a reference to the Work Package assigned). Quality tolerances will be defined in each Product Description
- **Schedule** Which may include graphical representations of:
  - Gantt or bar chart
  - Product breakdown structure
  - Product flow diagram
  - Activity network
  - Table of resource requirements – by resource type (e.g. four engineers, one test manager, one business analyst)
  - Table of requested/assigned specific resources – by name (e.g. Nikki, Jay, Francesca).

A.16.4 Format and presentation

A plan can take a number of formats, including:

- A stand-alone document or a section of the Project Initiation Documentation
- Document, spreadsheet, presentation slides or mindmap
- Entry in a project management tool.

The schedule may be in the form of a product checklist (which is a list of the products to be delivered within the scope of the plan, together with key status dates such as draft ready, quality inspected, approved etc.) or the output from a project planning tool.

A.16.5 Quality criteria

- The plan is achievable
- Estimates are based on consultation with the resources, who will undertake the work, and/or historical data
- Team Managers agree that their part of the plan is achievable
- It is planned to an appropriate level of detail (not too much, not too little)
- The plan conforms to required corporate or programme standards
- The plan incorporates lessons from previous projects
- The plan incorporates any legal requirements
- The plan covers management and control activities (such as quality) as well as the activities to create the products in scope
- The plan supports the Quality Management Strategy, Configuration Management Strategy, Risk Management Strategy, Communication Management Strategy and project approach
- The plan supports the management controls defined in the Project Initiation Documentation.

Table A.1 Example of a product checklist

Product identifier	Product title	Product Description approved		Draft ready		Final quality check completed		Approved		Handed over (if applicable)	
		Plan	Actual	Plan	Actual	Plan	Actual	Plan	Actual	Plan	Actual
...											
121	Test Plan	02/01	02/01	07/02	07/02	14/02	21/02	21/02	28/02	NA	NA
124	Water Pump	02/01	02/01	13/03	13/03	14/06		30/06		14/07	
...											

A.17 PRODUCT DESCRIPTION

A.17.1 Purpose

A Product Description is used to:

- Understand the detailed nature, purpose, function and appearance of the product
- Define who will use the product
- Identify the sources of information or supply for the product
- Identify the level of quality required of the product
- Enable identification of activities to produce, review and approve the product
- Define the people or skills required to produce, review and approve the product.

A.17.2 Composition

- **Identifier** Unique key, probably allocated by the configuration management method and likely to include the project name, item name and version number
- **Title** Name by which the product is known
- **Purpose** This defines the purpose that the product will fulfil and who will use it. Is it a means to an end or an end in itself? It is helpful in understanding the product's functions, size, quality, complexity, robustness etc.
- **Composition** This is a list of the parts of the product. For example, if the product were a report, this would be a list of the expected chapters or sections
- **Derivation** What are the source products from which this product is derived? Examples are:
  - A design is derived from a specification
  - A product is bought in from a supplier
  - A statement of the expected benefits is obtained from the user
  - A product is obtained from another department or team
- **Format and presentation** The characteristics of the product – for example, if the product were a report, this would specify whether the report should be a document, presentation slides or an email
- **Development skills required** An indication of the skills required to develop the product or a pointer to which area(s) should supply the development resources. Identification of the

actual people may be left until planning the stage in which the product is to be created

- **Quality criteria** To what quality specification must the product be produced, and what quality measurements will be applied by those inspecting the finished product? This might be a simple reference to one or more common standards that are documented elsewhere, or it might be a full explanation of some yardstick to be applied. If the product is to be developed and approved in different states (e.g. dismantled machinery, moved machinery and reassembled machinery), then the quality criteria should be grouped into those that apply for each state
- **Quality tolerance** Details of any range in the quality criteria within which the product would be acceptable
- **Quality method** The kinds of quality method – for example, design verification, pilot, test, inspection or review – that are to be used to check the quality or functionality of the product
- **Quality skills required** An indication of the skills required to undertake the quality method or a pointer to which area(s) should supply the checking resources. Identification of the actual people may be left until planning the stage in which the quality inspection is to be done
- **Quality responsibilities** Defining the producer, reviewer(s) and approver(s) for the product.

A.17.4 Format and presentation

A Product Description can take a number of formats, including:

- Document, presentation slides or mindmap
- Entry in a project management tool.

A.17.5 Quality criteria

- The purpose of the product is clear and is consistent with other products
- The product is described to a level of detail sufficient to plan and manage its development
- The Product Description is concise yet sufficient to enable the product to be produced, reviewed and approved
- Responsibility for the development of the product is clearly identified
- Responsibility for the development of the product is consistent with the roles and responsibilities described in the project

management team organization and the Quality Management Strategy

■ The quality criteria are consistent with the project quality standards, standard checklists and acceptance criteria

■ The quality criteria can be used to determine when the product is fit for purpose

■ The types of quality inspection required are able to verify whether the product meets its stated quality criteria

■ The Senior User(s) confirms that their requirements of the product, as defined in the Product Description, are accurately defined

■ The Senior Supplier(s) confirms that the requirements of the product, as defined in the Product Description, can be achieved.

A.19   PROJECT BRIEF

A.19.1 Purpose

A Project Brief is used to provide a full and firm foundation for the initiation of the project and is created in the Starting up a Project process.

In the Initiating a Project process, the contents of the Project Brief are extended and refined in the Project Initiation Documentation, after which the Project Brief is no longer maintained.

A.19.2 Composition

■ **Project definition** Explaining what the project needs to achieve. It should include:
  ● Background
  ● Project objectives (covering time, cost, quality, scope, risk and benefit performance goals)
  ● Desired outcomes
  ● Project scope and exclusions
  ● Constraints and assumptions
  ● Project tolerances
  ● The user(s) and any other known interested parties
  ● Interfaces
■ **Outline Business Case** (see section A.2) Reasons why the project is needed and the business option selected. This will later be developed into a detailed Business Case during the Initiating a Project process
■ **Project Product Description** (see section A.21) Including the customer's quality expectations,

user acceptance criteria, and operations and maintenance acceptance criteria

■ **Project approach** To define the choice of solution that will be used within the project to deliver the business option selected from the Business Case, taking into consideration the operational environment into which the solution must fit

■ **Project management team structure** A chart showing who will be involved with the project

■ **Role descriptions** For the project management team and any other key resources identified at this time

■ **References** To any associated documents or products.

A.19.4 Format and presentation

A Project Brief can take a number of formats, including:

■ Document or presentation slides
■ Entry in a project management tool.

A.19.5 Quality criteria

■ It is brief because its purpose at this point is to provide a firm basis on which to initiate a project. It will later be refined and expanded as part of the Project Initiation Documentation

■ The Project Brief accurately reflects the project mandate and the requirements of the business and the users

■ The project approach considers a range of solutions, such as: bespoke or off-the-shelf; contracted out or developed in-house; designed from new or a modified existing product

■ The project approach has been selected which maximizes the chance of achieving overall success for the project

■ The project objectives, project approach and strategies are consistent with the organization's corporate social responsibility directive

■ The project objectives are Specific, Measurable, Achievable, Realistic and Time-bound (SMART).

A.20   PROJECT INITIATION DOCUMENTATION

A.20.1 Purpose

The purpose of the Project Initiation Documentation is to define the project, in order to form the basis for its management and an assessment of its overall success. The Project Initiation Documentation gives the direction and scope of the project and (along with the Stage Plan) forms the 'contract' between the Project Manager and the Project Board.

The three primary uses of the Project Initiation Documentation are to:

■ Ensure that the project has a sound basis before asking the Project Board to make any major commitment to the project

■ Act as a base document against which the Project Board and Project Manager can assess progress, issues and ongoing viability questions

■ Provide a single source of reference about the project so that people joining the 'temporary organization' can quickly and easily find out what the project is about, and how it is being managed.

The Project Initiation Documentation is a living product in that it should always reflect the current status, plans and controls of the project. Its component products will need to be updated and re-baselined, as necessary, at the end of each stage, to reflect the current status of its constituent parts.

The version of the Project Initiation Documentation that was used to gain authorization for the project is preserved as the basis against which performance will later be assessed when closing the project.

A.20.2 Composition

There follows a contents list for the Project Initiation Documentation. Note that the first two (project definition and project approach) are extracted from the Project Brief.

■ **Project definition** Explaining what the project needs to achieve. It should include:
  ● Background
  ● Project objectives and desired outcomes
  ● Project scope and exclusions
  ● Constraints and assumptions
  ● The user(s) and any other known interested parties
  ● Interfaces

■ **Project approach** To define the choice of solution that will be used in the project to deliver the business option selected from the Business Case, taking into consideration

the operational environment into which the solution must fit

■ **Business Case** (see section A.2) Describing the justification for the project based on estimated costs, risks and benefits

■ **Project management team structure** A chart showing who will be involved with the project

■ **Role descriptions** For the project management team and any other key resources

■ **Quality Management Strategy** (see section A.22) Describing the quality techniques and standards to be applied, and the responsibilities for achieving the required quality levels

■ **Configuration Management Strategy** (see section A.6) Describing how and by whom the project's products will be controlled and protected

■ **Risk Management Strategy** (see section A.24) Describing the specific risk management techniques and standards to be applied, and the responsibilities for achieving an effective risk management procedure

■ **Communication Management Strategy** (see section A.4) To define the parties interested in the project and the means and frequency of communication between them and the project

■ **Project Plan** (see section A.16) Describing how and when the project's objectives are to be achieved, by showing the major products, activities and resources required on the project. It provides a baseline against which to monitor the project's progress stage by stage

■ **Project controls** Summarizing the project-level controls such as stage boundaries, agreed tolerances, monitoring and reporting

■ **Tailoring of PRINCE2** A summary of how PRINCE2 will be tailored for the project.

A.20.4 Format and presentation

The Project Initiation Documentation could be:

■ A single document

■ An index for a collection of documents

■ A document with cross-references to a number of other documents

■ A collection of information in a project management tool.

A.20.5 Quality criteria

■ The Project Initiation Documentation correctly represents the project

- It shows a viable, achievable project that is in line with corporate strategy or overall programme needs
- The project management team structure is complete, with names and titles. All the roles have been considered and are backed up by agreed role descriptions. The relationships and lines of authority are clear. If necessary, the project management team structure says to whom the Project Board reports
- It clearly shows a control, reporting and direction regime that can be implemented, appropriate to the scale, risk and importance of the project to corporate or programme management
- The controls cover the needs of the Project Board, Project Manager and Team Managers and satisfy any delegated assurance requirements
- It is clear who will administer each control
- The project objectives, approach and strategies are consistent with the organization's corporate social responsibility directive, and the project controls are adequate to ensure that the project remains compliant with such a directive
- Consideration has been given to the format of the Project Initiation Documentation. For small projects a single document is appropriate. For large projects it is more appropriate for the Project Initiation Documentation to be a collection of stand-alone documents. The volatility of each element of the Project Initiation Documentation should be used to assess whether it should be stand-alone, e.g. elements that are likely to change frequently are best separated out.

A.21 PROJECT PRODUCT DESCRIPTION

A.21.1 Purpose

The Project Product Description is a special form of Product Description that defines what the project must deliver in order to gain acceptance. It is used to:

- Gain agreement from the user on the project's scope and requirements
- Define the customer's quality expectations
- Define the acceptance criteria, method and responsibilities for the project.

The Project Product Description for the project product is created in the Starting up a Project process as part of the initial scoping activity, and is refined during the Initiating a Project process when creating the Project Plan. It is subject to formal change control and should be checked at stage boundaries (during Managing a Stage Boundary) to see if any changes are required. It is used by the Closing a Project process as part of the verification that the project has delivered what was expected of it, and that the acceptance criteria have been met.

A.21.2 Composition

- **Title** Name by which the project is known
- **Purpose** This defines the purpose that the project's product will fulfil and who will use it. It is helpful in understanding the product's functions, size, quality, complexity, robustness etc.
- **Composition** A description of the major products to be delivered by the project
- **Derivation** What are the source products from which this product is derived? Examples are:
  - Existing products to be modified
  - Design specifications
  - A feasibility report
  - Project mandate
- **Development skills required** An indication of the skills required to develop the product, or a pointer to which area(s) should supply the development resources
- **Customer's quality expectations** A description of the quality expected of the project's product and the standards and processes that will need to be applied to achieve that quality. They will impact on every part of the product development, and thus on time and cost. The quality expectations are captured in discussions with the customer. Where possible, expectations should be prioritized
- **Acceptance criteria** A prioritized list of criteria that the project's product must meet before the customer will accept it – i.e. measurable definitions of the attributes that must apply to the set of products to be acceptable to key stakeholders (and, in particular, the users and the operational and maintenance organizations). Examples are: ease of use, ease of support, ease of maintenance, appearance, major functions, development costs, running

costs, capacity, availability, reliability, security, accuracy or performance

- **Project-level quality tolerances** Specifying any tolerances that may apply for the acceptance criteria
- **Acceptance method** Stating the means by which acceptance will be confirmed. This may simply be a case of confirming that all the project's products have been approved or may involve describing complex handover arrangements for the project's product, including any phased handover of the project's products
- **Acceptance responsibilities** Defining who will be responsible for confirming acceptance.

A.21.4 Format and presentation

A Product Description for the project product can take a number of formats, including:

- Document, presentation slides or mindmap
- Entry in a project management tool.

A.21.5 Quality criteria

- The purpose is clear
- The composition defines the complete scope of the project
- The acceptance criteria form the complete list against which the project will be assessed
- The acceptance criteria address the requirements of all the key stakeholders (e.g. operations and maintenance)
- The Project Product Description defines how the users and the operational and maintenance organizations will assess the acceptability of the finished product(s):
  - All criteria are measurable
  - Each criterion is individually realistic
  - The criteria are realistic and consistent as a set. For example, high quality, early delivery and low cost may not go together
  - All criteria can be proven within the project life (e.g. the maximum throughput of a water pump), or by proxy measures that provide reasonable indicators as to whether acceptance criteria will be achieved post-project (e.g. a water pump that complies with design and manufacturing standards of reliability)
- The quality expectations have considered:

- The characteristics of the key quality requirements (e.g. fast/slow, large/small, national/global)
- The elements of the customer's quality management system that should be used
- Any other standards that should be used
- The level of customer/staff satisfaction that should be achieved if surveyed.

A.22 QUALITY MANAGEMENT STRATEGY

A.22.1 Purpose

A Quality Management Strategy is used to define the quality techniques and standards to be applied, and the various responsibilities for achieving the required quality levels, during the project.

A.22.2 Composition

- **Introduction** States the purpose, objectives and scope, and identifies who is responsible for the strategy
- **Quality management procedure** A description of (or reference to) the quality management procedure to be used. Any variance from corporate or programme management quality standards should be highlighted, together with a justification for the variance. The procedure should cover:
  - Quality planning
  - Quality control: the project's approach to quality control activities. This may include:
    - Quality standards
    - Templates and forms to be employed (e.g. Product Description(s), Quality Register)
    - Definitions of types of quality methods (e.g. inspection, pilot)
    - Metrics to be employed in support of quality control
  - Quality assurance: the project's approach to quality assurance activities. This may include:
    - Responsibilities of the Project Board
    - Compliance audits
    - Corporate or programme management reviews
- **Tools and techniques** Refers to any quality management systems or tools to be used, and any preference for techniques which may be used for each step in the quality management procedure

- **Records** Definition of what quality records will be required and where they will be stored, including the composition and format of the Quality Register
- **Reporting** Describes any quality management reports that are to produced, their purpose, timing and recipients
- **Timing of quality management activities** States when formal quality management activities are to be undertaken, for example audits (this may be a reference to the Quality Register)
- **Roles and responsibilities** Defines the roles and responsibilities for quality management activities, including those with quality responsibilities from corporate or programme management.

A.22.4 Format and presentation

A Quality Management Strategy can take a number of formats, including:

- Stand-alone document or a section of the Project Initiation Documentation
- Entry in a project management tool.

A.22.5 Quality criteria

- The strategy clearly defines ways in which the customer's quality expectations will be met
- The defined ways are sufficient to achieve the required quality
- Responsibilities for quality are defined up to a level that is independent of the project and Project Manager
- The strategy conforms to the supplier's and customer's quality management systems
- The strategy conforms to the corporate or programme quality policy
- The approaches to assuring quality for the project are appropriate in the light of the standards selected.

A.24 RISK MANAGEMENT STRATEGY

A.24.1 Purpose

A Risk Management Strategy describes the specific risk management techniques and standards to be applied and the responsibilities for achieving an effective risk management procedure.

A.24.2 Composition

- **Introduction** States the purpose, objectives and scope, and identifies who is responsible for the strategy
- **Risk management procedure** A description of (or reference to) the risk management procedure to be used. Any variance from corporate or programme management standards should be highlighted, together with a justification for the variance. The procedure should cover activities such as:
  - Identify
  - Assess
  - Plan
  - Implement
  - Communicate
- **Tools and techniques** Refers to any risk management systems or tools to be used, and any preference for techniques which may be used for each step in the risk management procedure
- **Records** Definition of the composition and format of the Risk Register and any other risk records to be used by the project
- **Reporting** Describes any risk management reports that are to be produced, including their purpose, timing and recipients
- **Timing of risk management activities** States when formal risk management activities are to be undertaken – for example, at end stage assessments
- **Roles and responsibilities** Defines the roles and responsibilities for risk management activities
- **Scales** Defines the scales for estimating probability and impact for the project to ensure that the scales for cost and time (for instance) are relevant to the cost and timeframe of the project. These may be shown in the form of probability impact grids giving the criteria for each level within the scale, e.g. for 'very high', 'high', 'medium', 'low' and 'very low'
- **Proximity** Guidance on how proximity for risk events is to be assessed. Proximity reflects the fact that risks will occur at particular times and the severity of their impact will vary according to when they occur. Typical proximity categories will be: imminent, within the stage, within the project, beyond the project
- **Risk categories** Definition of the risk categories to be used (if at all). These may be derived from

a risk breakdown structure or prompt list. If no risks have been recorded against a category, this may suggest that the risk identification has not been as thorough as it should have been

■ **Risk response categories** Definition of the risk response categories to be used, which themselves depend on whether a risk is a perceived threat or an opportunity

■ **Early-warning indicators** Definition of any indicators to be used to track critical aspects of the project so that if certain predefined levels are reached, corrective action will be triggered. They will be selected for their relevance to the project objectives

■ **Risk tolerance** Defining the threshold levels of risk exposure, which, when exceeded, require the risk to be escalated to the next level of management. (For example, a project-level risk tolerance could be set as any risk that, should it occur, would result in loss of trading. Such risks would need to be escalated to corporate or programme management.) The risk tolerance should define the risk expectations of corporate or programme management and the Project Board

■ **Risk budget** Describing whether a risk budget is to be established and, if so, how it will be used.

A.24.4 Format and presentation

A Risk Management Strategy can take a number of formats, including:

■ Stand-alone document or a section of the Project Initiation Documentation
■ Entry in a project management tool.

A.24.5 Quality criteria

■ Responsibilities are clear and understood by both customer and supplier
■ The risk management procedure is clearly documented and can be understood by all parties
■ Scales, expected value and proximity definitions are clear and unambiguous
■ The chosen scales are appropriate for the level of control required
■ Risk reporting requirements are fully defined.

A.26   WORK PACKAGE

A.26.1 Purpose

A Work Package is a set of information about one or more required products collated by the Project Manager to pass responsibility for work or delivery formally to a Team Manager or team member.

A.26.2 Composition

Although the content may vary greatly according to the relationship between the Project Manager and the recipient of the Work Package, it should cover:

■ **Date** The date of the agreement between the Project Manager and the Team Manager/person authorized

■ **Team Manager or person authorized** The name of the Team Manager or individual with whom the agreement has been made

■ **Work Package description** A description of the work to be done

■ **Techniques, processes and procedures** Any techniques, tools, standards, processes or procedures to be used in the creation of the specialist products

■ **Development interfaces** Interfaces that must be maintained while developing the products. These may be people providing information or those who need to receive information

■ **Operations and maintenance interfaces** Identification of any specialist products with which the product(s) in the Work Package will have to interface during their operational life. These may be other products to be produced by the project, existing products, or those to be produced by other projects (for example, if the project is part of a programme)

■ **Configuration management requirements** A statement of any arrangements that must be made by the producer for: version control of the products in the Work Package; obtaining copies of other products or their Product Descriptions; submission of the product to configuration management; any storage or security requirements; and who, if anyone, needs to be advised of changes in the status of the Work Package

■ **Joint agreements** Details of the agreements on effort, cost, start and end dates, and key milestones for the Work Package

- **Tolerances** Details of the tolerances for the Work Package (the tolerances will be for time and cost but may also include scope and risk)
- **Constraints** Any constraints (apart from the tolerances) on the work, people to be involved, timings, charges, rules to be followed (for example, security and safety) etc.
- **Reporting arrangements** The expected frequency and content of Checkpoint Reports
- **Problem handling and escalation** This refers to the procedure for raising issues and risks
- **Extracts or references** Any extracts or references to related documents, specifically:
  - **Stage Plan extract** This will be the relevant section of the Stage Plan for the current management stage or will be a pointer to it
  - **Product Description(s)** This would normally be an attachment of the Product Description(s) for the products identified in the Work Package (note that the Product Description contains the quality methods to be used)
- **Approval method** The person, role or group who will approve the completed products within the Work Package, and how the Project Manager is to be advised of completion of the products and Work Package.

There should be space on the Work Package to record both its initial authorization and its acceptance and return as a completed Work Package. This can be enhanced to include an assessment of the work and go towards performance appraisal.

Projects with common controls across all Work Packages may simply cross-reference the controls defined in the Project Plan or Stage Plan.

A.26.4 Format and presentation

A Work Package can take a number of formats, including:

- Document
- Oral conversation between the Project Manager and a Team Manager
- Entry in a project management tool.

The Work Package will vary in content and in degree of formality, depending on circumstances.

Where the work is being conducted by a team working directly under the Project Manager, the Work Package may be an oral instruction – although there are good reasons for putting it in writing, such as avoidance of misunderstanding and providing a link to performance assessment. Where the work is being carried out by a supplier under a contract and the Project Manager is part of the customer organization, there is a need for a formal written instruction in line with standards laid down in that contract.

A.26.5 Quality criteria

- The required Work Package is clearly defined and understood by the assigned resource
- There is a Product Description for each required product, with clearly identified and acceptable quality criteria
- The Product Description(s) matches up with the other Work Package documentation
- Standards for the work are agreed
- The defined standards are in line with those applied to similar products
- All necessary interfaces have been defined
- The reporting arrangements include the provision for raising issues and risks
- There is agreement between the Project Manager and the recipient on exactly what is to be done
- There is agreement on the constraints, including effort, cost and targets
- The dates and effort are in line with those shown in the Stage Plan for the current management stage
- Reporting arrangements are defined
- Any requirement for independent attendance at, and participation in, quality activities is defined.

Appendix B: Governance

Appendix B: Governance

The governance of project management concerns those areas of corporate governance that are specifically related to project activities. Effective governance of project management ensures that an organization's project portfolio is aligned to the organization's objectives, is delivered efficiently, and is sustainable. Governance of project management also supports the means by which the corporate board and other major project stakeholders are provided with timely, relevant and reliable information.

Table B.1 The Association for Project Management's governance of project management principles

Governance of project management principles	Addressed by PRINCE2?
The board has overall responsibility for governance of project management.	This governance principle relates to the main board of the corporate organization and is outside the scope of PRINCE2.
The roles, responsibilities and performance criteria for the governance of project management are clearly defined.	Partially. The project has clearly defined roles, responsibilities and performance criteria for governance, but PRINCE2 does not extend into the governance responsibilities of the corporate roles.
Disciplined governance arrangements, supported by appropriate methods and controls, are applied throughout the project lifecycle.	Fully.
A coherent and supportive relationship is demonstrated between the overall business strategy and the project portfolio.	Partially. Each PRINCE2 project should demonstrate alignment to corporate strategy through its Business Case. PRINCE2 does not provide guidance on portfolio management.
All projects have an approved plan containing authorization points at which the Business Case is reviewed and approved. Decisions made at authorization points are recorded and communicated.	Fully.
Members of delegated authorization bodies have sufficient representation, competence, authority and resources to enable them to make appropriate decisions.	Partially. PRINCE2 provides the framework for effective delegation. The competence of project personnel is outside the scope of PRINCE2.
The project Business Case is supported by relevant and realistic information that provides a reliable basis for making authorization decisions.	Fully.
The board, or its delegated agents, decide when independent scrutiny of projects and project management systems is required, and implement such scrutiny accordingly.	Partially. PRINCE2 recommends independent scrutiny by corporate or programme management as part of the Project Assurance responsibilities.
There are clearly defined criteria for reporting project status, and for the escalation of risks and issues to the levels required by the organization.	Fully.
The organization fosters a culture of improvement and of frank internal disclosure of project information.	Partially. PRINCE2 encourages open reporting through its management-by-exception and assurance structures.
Project stakeholders are engaged at a level that is commensurate with their importance to the organization, and in a manner that fosters trust.	Fully.

From *Directing Change: A Guide to Governance of Project Management* (reprinted with minor revisions 2005), APM Governance SIG. © Association for Project Management, 2004. Reproduced with permission.

PRINCE2 provides (if applied within the spirit of its principles) a framework for effective governance. Table B.1 shows how PRINCE2 addresses the governance principles published by the Association for Project Management.

Appendix C:
Roles and responsibilities

Appendix C: Roles and responsibilities

C.1 PROJECT BOARD

The Project Board is accountable to corporate or programme management for the success of the project, and has the authority to direct the project within the remit set by corporate or programme management as documented in the project mandate.

The Project Board is also responsible for the communications between the project management team and stakeholders external to that team (e.g. corporate and programme management).

According to the scale, complexity, importance and risk of the project, Project Board members may delegate some Project Assurance tasks to separate individuals. The Project Board may also delegate decisions regarding changes to a Change Authority.

C.1.1 General responsibilities

During start-up and initiation:

- Confirm project tolerances with corporate or programme management
- Approve the Project Brief
- Approve the Stage Plan for the initiation stage
- Authorize project initiation
- Decide whether to use a Change Authority and, if so, agree the level of authority to be delegated
- Set the scale for severity ratings for issues
- Set the scale for priority ratings for requests for change and off-specifications
- Approve the supplier contract (if the relationship between the customer and supplier is a commercial one)
- Approve the Project Initiation Documentation (and its components)
- Authorize the start of the project.

During the project:

- Set tolerances for each stage and approve Stage Plans
- Authorize each management stage and approve the Product Descriptions for each stage
- Approve Exception Plans when stage-level tolerances are forecast to be exceeded

- Communicate with stakeholders as defined in the Communication Management Strategy (including briefing corporate or programme management about project progress)
- Provide overall guidance and direction to the project, ensuring it remains viable and within any specified constraints
- Respond to requests for advice from the Project Manager
- Ensure that risks are being tracked and managed as effectively as possible
- Approve changes (unless delegated to a Change Authority)
- Make decisions on escalated issues
- Approve completed products.

At the end of the project:

- Provide assurance that all products have been delivered satisfactorily
- Provide assurance that all acceptance criteria have been met
- Confirm acceptance of the project product
- Approve the End Project Report and ensure that any issues, lessons and risks are documented and passed on to the appropriate body
- Authorize follow-on action recommendations and Lessons Reports to be distributed to corporate or programme management
- Transfer responsibility for the updated Benefits Review Plan to corporate or programme management
- Authorize project closure and send project closure notification to corporate or programme management.

C.1.2 Competencies

To be successful, the Project Board should:

- Have sufficient authority to make decisions, approve plans and authorize any necessary deviation from Stage Plans
- Have sufficient authority to allocate resources to the project
- Be capable of adequately representing the business, user and supplier interests

- Ideally be able to stay with the project throughout its life.

Key competencies include:

- Decision making
- Delegation
- Leadership
- Negotiation and conflict resolution.

C.2 EXECUTIVE

The Executive is ultimately responsible for the project, supported by the Senior User and Senior Supplier. The Executive's role is to ensure that the project is focused throughout its life on achieving its objectives and delivering a product that will achieve the forecast benefits. The Executive has to ensure that the project gives value for money, ensuring a cost-conscious approach to the project, balancing the demands of the business, user and supplier.

Throughout the project, the Executive is responsible for the Business Case.

The Project Board is not a democracy controlled by votes. The Executive is the ultimate decision maker and is supported in the decision making by the Senior User and Senior Supplier.

C.2.1 Responsibilities

In addition to the Project Board's collective responsibilities, the Executive will:

- Design and appoint the project management team (in particular the Project Manager)
- Oversee the development of the Project Brief and the outline Business Case, ensuring that the project is aligned with corporate strategies (and presenting the outline Business Case to corporate or programme management for approval where required)
- Oversee the development of the detailed Business Case
- Secure the funding for the project
- Approve any additional supplier contracts (if the relationship between the user and supplier is a commercial one)
- Hold the Senior Supplier to account for the quality and integrity of the specialist approach and specialist products created for the project
- Hold the Senior User to account for realizing the benefits defined in the Business Case,

ensuring that benefits reviews take place to monitor the extent to which the Business Case benefits are achieved
- Transfer responsibility for post-project benefits reviews to corporate or programme management
- Monitor and control the progress of the project at a strategic level, in particular reviewing the Business Case regularly
- Escalate issues and risks to corporate or programme management if project tolerance is forecast to be exceeded
- Ensure that risks associated with the Business Case are identified, assessed and controlled
- Make decisions on escalated issues, with particular focus on continued business justification
- Organize and chair Project Board reviews
- Ensure overall business assurance of the project – that it remains on target to deliver products that will achieve the expected business benefits, and that the project will be completed within its agreed tolerances. Where appropriate, delegate some business Project Assurance activities (see section C.7).

C.3 SENIOR USER

The Senior User(s) is responsible for specifying the needs of those who will use the project's products, for user liaison with the project management team, and for monitoring that the solution will meet those needs within the constraints of the Business Case in terms of quality, functionality and ease of use.

The role represents the interests of all those who will use the project's products (including operations and maintenance), those for whom the products will achieve an objective or those who will use the products to deliver benefits. The Senior User role commits user resources and monitors products against requirements. This role may require more than one person to cover all the user interests. For the sake of effectiveness, the role should not be split between too many people.

The Senior User(s) specifies the benefits and is held to account by demonstrating to corporate or programme management that the forecast benefits which were the basis of project approval have in fact been realized. This is likely to involve a commitment beyond the end of the life of the project.

C.3.1 Responsibilities

In addition to the Project Board's collective responsibilities, the Senior User(s) will:

- Provide the customer's quality expectations and define acceptance criteria for the project
- Ensure that the desired outcome of the project is specified
- Ensure that the project produces products that will deliver the desired outcomes, and meet user requirements
- Ensure that the expected benefits (derived from the project's outcomes) are realized
- Provide a statement of actual versus forecast benefits at the benefits reviews
- Resolve user requirements and priority conflicts
- Ensure that any user resources required for the project (e.g. to undertake user quality inspections and product approval) are made available
- Make decisions on escalated issues, with particular focus on safeguarding the expected benefits
- Brief and advise user management on all matters concerning the project
- Maintain business performance stability during transition from the project to business as usual
- Provide the user view on follow-on action recommendations
- Undertake Project Assurance from the user perspective (user assurance) and, where appropriate, delegate user Project Assurance activities (see section C.7).

C.4 SENIOR SUPPLIER

The Senior Supplier represents the interests of those designing, developing, facilitating, procuring and implementing the project's products. This role is accountable for the quality of products delivered by the supplier(s) and is responsible for the technical integrity of the project. If necessary, more than one person may be required to represent the suppliers.

Depending on the particular customer/supplier environment, the customer may also wish to appoint an independent person or group to carry out assurance on the supplier's products (for example, if the relationship between the customer and supplier is a commercial one).

C.4.1 Responsibilities

In addition to the Project Board's collective responsibilities, the Senior Supplier will:

- Assess and confirm the viability of the project approach
- Ensure that proposals for designing and developing the products are realistic
- Advise on the selection of design, development and acceptance methods
- Ensure that the supplier resources required for the project are made available
- Make decisions on escalated issues, with particular focus on safeguarding the integrity of the complete solution
- Resolve supplier requirements and priority conflicts
- Brief non-technical management on supplier aspects of the project
- Ensure quality procedures are used correctly, so that products adhere to requirements
- Undertake Project Assurance from the supplier perspective (supplier assurance) and, where appropriate, delegate supplier Project Assurance activities (see section C.7).

C.5 PROJECT MANAGER

The Project Manager has the authority to run the project on a day-to-day basis on behalf of the Project Board within the constraints laid down by them.

The Project Manager's prime responsibility is to ensure that the project produces the required products within the specified tolerances of time, cost, quality, scope, risk and benefits. The Project Manager is also responsible for the project producing a result capable of achieving the benefits defined in the Business Case.

C.5.1 Responsibilities

The Project Manager's responsibilities include the following:

- Prepare the following baseline management products, in conjunction with any Project Assurance roles, and agree them with the Project Board:
  - Project Brief, including the Project Product Description
  - Benefits Review Plan

- Project Initiation Documentation (and its components)
- Stage/Exception Plans and their Product Descriptions
- Work Packages

■ Prepare the following reports:
  - Highlight Reports
  - Issue Reports
  - End Stage Reports
  - Lessons Reports
  - Exception Reports
  - End Project Report

■ Maintain the following records:
  - Issue Register
  - Risk Register
  - Daily Log
  - Lessons Log

■ Liaise with corporate or programme management to ensure that work is neither overlooked nor duplicated by related projects

■ Liaise with any external suppliers or account managers

■ Lead and motivate the project management team

■ Ensure that behavioural expectations of team members are established

■ Manage the information flows between the directing and delivering levels of the project

■ Manage the production of the required products, taking responsibility for overall progress and use of resources and initiating corrective action where necessary

■ Establish and manage the project's procedures – risk management, issue and change control, configuration management, and communication

■ Establish and manage the project controls – monitoring and reporting

■ Authorize Work Packages

■ Advise the Project Board of any deviations from the plan

■ Unless appointed to another person(s), perform the Team Manager role (see section C.6)

■ Unless appointed to another person (or corporate/programme function), perform the Project Support role (see section C.9)

■ Implement the Configuration Management Strategy

■ Ensure project personnel comply with the Configuration Management Strategy

■ Schedule configuration audits to check that the physical products are consistent with the Configuration Item Records and initiate any necessary corrective action.

C.5.2 Competencies

Different types of project will require different types of project management skills. To be successful, the Project Manager must be able to balance the different aspects of the Project Manager role for a particular project.

Key competencies include:

■ Planning
■ Time management
■ People management
■ Problem solving
■ Attention to detail
■ Communication
■ Negotiation
■ Conflict management.

C.6 TEAM MANAGER

The Team Manager's prime responsibility is to ensure production of those products defined by the Project Manager to an appropriate quality, within a set timescale and at a cost acceptable to the Project Board. The Team Manager role reports to, and takes direction from, the Project Manager.

C.7 PROJECT ASSURANCE

Project Assurance covers the primary stakeholder interests (business, user and supplier).

Project Assurance has to be independent of the Project Manager; therefore the Project Board cannot delegate any of its assurance activities to the Project Manager.

C.7.1 Responsibilities

The implementation of the assurance responsibilities needs to answer the question: what is to be assured? A list of possibilities applicable to the business, user and supplier stakeholder interests would include ensuring that:

■ Liaison is maintained between the business, user and supplier throughout the project

- Risks are controlled
- The right people are involved in writing Product Descriptions
- The right people are planned to be involved in quality inspection at the correct points in the products' development
- Staff are properly trained in the quality methods
- The quality methods are being correctly followed
- Quality control follow-up actions are dealt with correctly
- An acceptable solution is being developed
- The scope of the project is not changing unnoticed
- Internal and external communications are working
- Applicable standards are being used
- The needs of specialist interests (for example, security) are being observed.

Business assurance responsibilities

- Assist the Project Manager to develop the Business Case and Benefits Review Plan (if it is being prepared by the Project Manager)
- Advise on the selection of project management team members
- Advise on the Risk Management Strategy
- Review the Business Case for compliance with corporate or programme standards
- Verify the Business Case against external events and against project progress
- Check that the Business Case is being adhered to throughout the project
- Check that the project remains aligned to the corporate or programme strategy
- Review project finance on behalf of the customer
- Verify that the solution continues to provide value for money
- Periodically check that the project remains viable
- Assess that the aggregated risk exposure remains within project tolerance
- Check that any supplier and contractor payments are authorized
- Review issues and risks by assessing their impact on the Business Case
- Constrain user and supplier excesses

- Inform the project management team of any changes caused by a programme of which the project is part (this responsibility may be transferred if there is other programme representation on the project management team)
- Monitor stage and project progress against the agreed tolerances.

User assurance responsibilities

- Advise on stakeholder engagement
- Advise on the Communication Management Strategy
- Ensure that the specification of the user's needs is accurate, complete and unambiguous
- Assess whether the solution will meet the user's needs and is progressing towards that target
- Advise on the impact of potential changes from the user's point of view
- Monitor risks to the user
- Ensure that the quality activities relating to products at all stages has appropriate user representation
- Ensure that quality control procedures are used correctly to ensure that products meet user requirements
- Ensure that user liaison is functioning effectively.

Supplier assurance responsibilities

- Review the Product Descriptions
- Advise on the Quality Management Strategy and Configuration Management Strategy
- Advise on the selection of the development strategy, design and methods
- Ensure that any supplier and operating standards defined for the project are met and used to good effect
- Advise on potential changes and their impact on the correctness, completeness and integrity of products against their Product Description from a supplier perspective
- Monitor any risks in the production aspects of the project
- Assess whether quality control procedures are used correctly, so that products adhere to requirements.

C.7.2 Competencies

To be successful, Project Assurance should:

- Be capable of adequately representing the business, user or supplier stakeholder interests
- Have sufficient credibility to ensure that advice and guidance are followed
- Have sufficient specialist knowledge of the business, user or supplier stakeholder areas
- Ideally be able to stay with the project throughout its lifecycle.

Key competencies include:

- Diplomacy
- Thoroughness
- Attention to detail
- Communication.

C.8   CHANGE AUTHORITY

The Project Board may delegate authority for approving responses to requests for change or off-specifications to a separate individual or group, called a Change Authority. The Project Manager could be assigned as the Change Authority for some aspects of the project (e.g. changing baselined Work Packages if it does not affect stage tolerances).

C.8.1 Responsibilities

- Review and approve or reject all requests for change and off-specifications within the delegated limits of authority and change budget set by the Project Board
- Refer to the Project Board if any delegated limits of authority or allocated change budget are forecast to be exceeded.

C.8.2 Competencies

The Change Authority should:

- Be capable of adequately representing the business, user and supplier stakeholder interests
- Have sufficient credibility to ensure that advice and guidance are followed
- Have sufficient specialist knowledge of the business, user or supplier stakeholder areas.

Key competencies include:

- Decision making
- Planning
- Attention to detail
- Problem solving.

C.9   PROJECT SUPPORT

The provision of any Project Support on a formal basis is optional. If it is not delegated to a separate person or function it will need to be undertaken by the Project Manager.

One support function that must be considered is that of configuration management. Depending on the project size and environment, there may be a need to formalize this and it may become a task with which the Project Manager cannot cope without support.

Project Support functions may be provided by a project office or by specific resources for the project. Refer to OGC's guidance *Portfolio, Programme and Project Offices* (TSO, 2008) for further information on the use of a project office.

Further information

Further information

FROM THE OFFICE OF GOVERNMENT COMMERCE

PRINCE2

PRINCE2 is part of a suite of guidance developed by the Office of Government Commerce (OGC), aimed at helping organizations and individuals manage their projects, programmes and services. Where appropriate, this guidance is supported by a qualification scheme and accredited training and consultancy services.

Managing Successful Projects with PRINCE2 (2009). The Stationery Office, London.

Directing Successful Projects with PRINCE2 (2009). The Stationery Office, London.

Management of Risk (M_o_R®)

Projects exist in a fundamentally uncertain world and, as such, effective management of risk is crucial to managing the delivery of the project's products, their outcomes and the ultimate benefits that have been identified. Management of risk (M_o_R) puts the management of project risk into the context of the wider business environment.

Management of Risk: Guidance for Practitioners (2007). The Stationery Office, London.

Managing Successful Programmes

Managing Successful Programmes (MSP) represents proven programme management good practice in successfully delivering transformational change across a wide range of public and private sector organizations. It provides a framework to direct and oversee the implementation of a set of related projects and activities in order to deliver outcomes and benefits related to the organization's strategic objectives.

Managing Successful Programmes (2007). The Stationery Office, London.

Portfolio Management Guide

The Portfolio Management Guide explains the key principles of portfolio management, from the experience of public and private sector organizations in the UK and internationally. It provides practical advice on setting up a portfolio management function, illustrated with real-life examples, and concludes with a section on further advice and guidance. The main audience for this guide comprises the teams responsible for coordinating programmes and projects, particularly those providing support for investment decisions and reporting on progress to the management board. A working knowledge of programme and project management and progress reporting is assumed.

Portfolio, Programme and Project Management Maturity Model (P3M3™)

The Portfolio, Programme and Project Management Maturity Model (P3M3) is a reference guide for structured best practice. It breaks down the broad disciplines of portfolio, programme and project management into a hierarchy of perspectives.

The hierarchical approach enables organizations to assess their current capability and then plot a roadmap for improvement prioritized by those perspectives that will make the biggest impact on performance.

Portfolio, Programme and Project Offices

Portfolio, Programme and Project Offices (P3O®) provides guidance on how to define, establish and operate a portfolio, programme or project office. It covers the range of functions and services that P3Os may provide and includes references to the techniques that may be employed.

Portfolio, Programme and Project Offices (2008). The Stationery Office, London.

PRINCE2 Maturity Model (P2MM)

The PRINCE2 Maturity Model (P2MM) describes a set of key process areas (KPAs) required for the effective implementation and use of PRINCE2 within an organization. This is P2MM's core value: while the PRINCE2 manual describes how to manage a single project, it does not include any processes on how to embed PRINCE2, whereas P2MM does.

P2MM describes key practices aligned with the PRINCE2 processes and components to enable repeatable application of the method (Level 2), and goes further to describe the key practices required to institutionalize the method (Level 3) as a standard business process for managing projects.

OGC Gateway Review process

OGC Gateway Review process is a well-established project and programme assurance review process which is mandated for all UK government high-risk programmes and projects. OGC Gateway Review delivers a peer review, in which independent practitioners from outside the individual programme/project use their experience and expertise to examine progress and assess the likelihood of successful delivery of the programme or project. The review process is used to provide a valuable additional perspective on the issues facing the internal team, and an external challenge to the robustness of plans and processes. This service is based on good practice and there are many similar examples across all business sectors of this type of peer review designed to provide assurance to the owner of the programme or project.

Full details of the OGC Gateway Review process are available from the OGC website.

Achieving Excellence in Construction

Achieving Excellence in Construction procurement guidance is contained within a set of 11 guides and two high-level guides. It builds on UK central government departments' recent experience, supports future strategy and aligns with the OGC Gateway Review process.

Through the Achieving Excellence in Construction initiative, central government departments and public sector organizations commit to maximize, by continual improvement, the efficiency, effectiveness and value for money of their procurement of new works, maintenance and refurbishment.

ITIL® Service Management Practices

ITIL is the most widely accepted approach to IT service management in the world. Providing a cohesive set of best-practice guidance drawn from the public and private sectors across the world, it

has recently undergone a major and important refresh project.

IT Service Management (ITSM) derives enormous benefits from a best-practice approach. Because ITSM is driven both by technology and the huge range of organizational environments in which it operates, it is in a state of constant evolution. Best practice, based on expert advice and input from ITIL users, is both current and practical, combining the latest thinking with sound, common-sense guidance.

Continual Service Improvement (2007). The Stationery Office, London.

Service Design (2007). The Stationery Office, London.

Service Operation (2007). The Stationery Office, London.

Service Strategy (2007). The Stationery Office, London.

Service Transition (2007). The Stationery Office, London.

FROM THE STATIONERY OFFICE (COMPLEMENTARY PUBLICATIONS)

APMP for PRINCE2 Practitioners

This study guide enables candidates familiar with PRINCE2 to prepare for the APMP exam. It provides APMP exam candidates with a single source of reference material that covers all aspects of the APMP syllabus, including both pre-course and on-course material, whilst aligning it with the PRINCE2 method. This enables PRINCE2 practitioners (or project management staff working within a PRINCE2 environment) to expand their project management knowledge to cover all topics within the APMP syllabus.

APMP for PRINCE2 Practitioners (2008). The Stationery Office, London.

Focus on Skills series suite (set of three books)

The Focus on Skills series suite explores the various 'soft skills' that are demonstrated by effective project and programme managers, as the day-to-day coordination, motivation and communication aspects of project and programme management are very similar.

Leadership Skills for Project and Programme Managers (2008). The Stationery Office, London.

Team Management Skills for Project and Programme Managers (2008). The Stationery Office, London.

Communication Skills for Project and Programme Managers (2008). The Stationery Office, London.

Agile Project Management: Running PRINCE2 Projects with DSDM Atern

This ground-breaking book shows how users can combine the strength of both approaches considered, so that they complement each other and create a new, best-of-breed framework suitable for all project environments. Based on PRINCE2 and DSDM Atern, the two most established and internationally recognized project management approaches, this title explores the differences between the two approaches before showing where they overlap and how they can be integrated. While DSDM Atern is a project management methodology in its own right, this new publication sits within the PRINCE2 suite of titles.

Agile Project Management: Running PRINCE2 Projects with DSDM Atern (2007). The Stationery Office, London.

Improving Project Performance using the PRINCE2 Maturity Model

PRINCE2 is cited as the most widely used project management method worldwide, but, while the PRINCE2 manual describes how to manage a single project, it does not include any guidance on how to embed PRINCE2 into an organization.

Such guidance is now available: this publication describes the organizational processes and practices required for the effective implementation of PRINCE2 as an organizational standard. It includes guidance on assigning ownership, tailoring the method, training, integrating PRINCE2 with other management systems and establishing quality assurance mechanisms to gain a continual improvement capability.

In reading *Improving Project Performance using the PRINCE2 Maturity Model*, you will discover how organizations can gain full value from the PRINCE2 method. It contains practical advice on using the

OGC's PRINCE2 Maturity Model (P2MM), and shows how P2MM can be applied in different situations.

Improving Project Performance using the PRINCE2 Maturity Model (2007). The Stationery Office, London.

OTHER SOURCES

The following is a list of useful references, some of which have been cited by the PRINCE2 authors.

Adair, John (2004) *The John Adair Handbook of Management and Leadership*, Thorogood, ISBN 978-1854182043.

APM GoPM Specific Interest Group (2005) *Directing Change: A Guide to the Governance of Project Management*, 2nd edition, Association for Project Management, High Wycombe, ISBN 1-903494-15-X.

Association of Project Management (2006) *APM Body of Knowledge*, 5th edition, High Wycombe, ISBN 978-1903494134.

British Standards Institution (2002) *BS6079–1:2002 A Guide to Project Management*, BSI, London.

Goldratt, Eliyahu M. (1997) *Critical Chain*, Avebury, ISBN 978-0566080388.

International Project Management Association (2006) *ICB-IPMA Competency Baseline, version 3.0*, ISBN 0-9553213-0-1.

Project Management Institute (2004) *A Guide to the Project Management Body of Knowledge: PMBOK Guide*, 3rd edition, ISBN 978-1930699458.

Winter, Mark and Smith, Charles (2006) *Rethinking Project Management*, EPSRC Network 2004–2006.

Glossary

Glossary

accept (risk response)

A risk response to a threat where a conscious and deliberate decision is taken to retain the threat, having discerned that it is more economical to do so than to attempt a risk response action. The threat should continue to be monitored to ensure that it remains tolerable.

acceptance

The formal act of acknowledging that the project has met agreed acceptance criteria and thereby met the requirements of its stakeholders.

acceptance criteria

A prioritized list of criteria that the project product must meet before the customer will accept it, i.e. measurable definitions of the attributes required for the set of products to be acceptable to key stakeholders.

activity

A process, function or task that occurs over time, has recognizable results and is managed. It is usually defined as part of a process or plan.

agile methods

Principally, software development methods that apply the project approach of using short time-boxed iterations where products are incrementally developed. PRINCE2 is compatible with agile principles.

approval

The formal confirmation that a product is complete and meets its requirements (less any concessions) as defined by its Product Description.

approver

The person or group (e.g. a Project Board) who is identified as qualified and authorized to approve a (management or specialist) product as being complete and fit for purpose.

assumption

A statement that is taken as being true for the purposes of planning, but which could change later. An assumption is made where some facts are not yet known or decided, and is usually reserved for matters of such significance that, if they change or turn out not to be true, there will need to be considerable replanning.

assurance

All the systematic actions necessary to provide confidence that the target (system, process, organization, programme, project, outcome, benefit, capability, product output, deliverable) is appropriate. Appropriateness might be defined subjectively or objectively in different circumstances. The implication is that assurance will have a level of independence from that which is being assured. See also 'Project Assurance' and 'quality assurance'.

authority

The right to allocate resources and make decisions (applies to project, stage and team levels).

authorization

The point at which an authority is granted.

avoid (risk response)

A risk response to a threat where the threat either can no longer have an impact or can no longer happen.

baseline

Reference levels against which an entity is monitored and controlled.

baseline management product

A type of management product that defines aspects of the project and, once approved, is subject to change control.

benefit

The measurable improvement resulting from an outcome perceived as an advantage by one or more stakeholders.

Benefits Review Plan

A plan that defines how and when a measurement of the achievement of the project's benefits can be made. If the project is being managed within a programme, this information may be created and maintained at the programme level.

benefits tolerance

The permissible deviation in the expected benefit that is allowed before the deviation needs to be escalated to the next level of management. Benefits tolerance is documented in the Business Case. See also 'tolerance'.

Business Case

The justification for an organizational activity (project), which typically contains costs, benefits, risks and timescales, and against which continuing viability is tested.

centre of excellence

A corporate coordinating function for portfolios, programmes and projects providing standards, consistency of methods and processes, knowledge management, assurance and training.

Change Authority

A person or group to which the Project Board may delegate responsibility for the consideration of requests for change or off-specifications. The Change Authority may be given a change budget and can approve changes within that budget.

change budget

The money allocated to the Change Authority available to be spent on authorized requests for change.

change control

The procedure that ensures that all changes that may affect the project's agreed objectives are identified, assessed and either approved, rejected or deferred.

checkpoint

A team-level, time-driven review of progress.

Checkpoint Report

A progress report of the information gathered at a checkpoint, which is given by a team to the Project Manager and which provides reporting data as defined in the Work Package.

closure notification

Advice from the Project Board to inform all stakeholders and the host sites that the project resources can be disbanded and support services, such as space, equipment and access, demobilized. It should indicate a closure date for costs to be charged to the project.

closure recommendation

A recommendation prepared by the Project Manager for the Project Board to send as a project closure notification when the board is satisfied that the project can be closed.

Communication Management Strategy

A description of the means and frequency of communication between the project and the project's stakeholders.

concession

An off-specification that is accepted by the Project Board without corrective action.

configuration item

An entity that is subject to configuration management. The entity may be a component of a product, a product, or a set of products in a release.

Configuration Item Record

A record that describes the status, version and variant of a configuration item, and any details of important relationships between them.

configuration management

Technical and administrative activities concerned with the creation, maintenance and controlled change of configuration throughout the life of a product.

Configuration Management Strategy

A description of how and by whom the project's products will be controlled and protected.

configuration management system

The set of processes, tools and databases that are used to manage configuration data. Typically, a project will use the configuration management system of either the customer or supplier organization.

constraints

The restrictions or limitations that the project is bound by.

contingency

Something that is held in reserve typically to handle time and cost variances, or risks. PRINCE2 does not advocate the use of contingency because estimating variances are managed by setting tolerances, and risks are managed through appropriate risk responses (including the fallback response that is contingent on the risk occurring).

corporate or programme standards

These are over-arching standards that the project must adhere to. They will influence the four project strategies (Communication Management Strategy, Configuration Management Strategy, Quality Management Strategy and Risk Management Strategy) and the project controls.

corrective action

A set of actions to resolve a threat to a plan's tolerances or a defect in a product.

cost tolerance

The permissible deviation in a plan's cost that is allowed before the deviation needs to be escalated to the next level of management. Cost tolerance is documented in the respective plan. See also 'tolerance'.

customer

The person or group who commissioned the work and will benefit from the end results.

customer's quality expectations

A statement about the quality expected from the project product, captured in the Project Product Description.

Daily Log

Used to record problems/concerns that can be handled by the Project Manager informally.

deliverable

See 'output'.

dependencies (plan)

The relationship between products or activities. For example, the development of Product C cannot start until Products A and B have been completed. Dependencies can be internal or external.

Internal dependencies are those under the control of the Project Manager. External dependencies are those outside the control of the Project Manager – for example, the delivery of a product required by this project from another project.

dis-benefit

An outcome that is perceived as negative by one or more stakeholders. It is an actual consequence of an activity whereas, by definition, a risk has some uncertainty about whether it will materialize.

DSDM Atern

An agile project delivery framework developed and owned by the DSDM consortium. Atern uses a time-boxed and iterative approach to product development and is compatible with PRINCE2.

embedding (PRINCE2)

What an organization needs to do to adopt PRINCE2 as its corporate project management method. See also, in contrast, 'tailoring', which defines what a project needs to do to apply the method to a specific project environment.

End Project Report

A report given by the Project Manager to the Project Board, that confirms the handover of all products and provides an updated Business Case and an assessment of how well the project has done against the original Project Initiation Documentation.

end stage assessment

The review by the Project Board and Project Manager of the End Stage Report to decide whether to approve the next Stage Plan. According to the size and criticality of the project, the review may be formal or informal. The authority to proceed should be documented as a formal record.

End Stage Report

A report given by the Project Manager to the Project Board at the end of each management stage of the project. This provides information about the project performance during the stage and the project status at stage end.

enhance (risk response)

A risk response to an opportunity where proactive actions are taken to enhance both the probability of the event occurring and the impact of the event should it occur.

event-driven control

A control that takes place when a specific event occurs. This could be, for example, the end of a stage, the completion of the Project Initiation Documentation, or the creation of an Exception Report. It could also include organizational events that may affect the project, such as the end of the financial year.

exception

A situation where it can be forecast that there will be a deviation beyond the tolerance levels agreed between Project Manager and Project Board (or between Project Board and corporate or programme management).

exception assessment

This is a review by the Project Board to approve (or reject) an Exception Plan.

Exception Plan

This is a plan that often follows an Exception Report. For a Stage Plan exception, it covers the period from the present to the end of the current stage. If the exception were at project level, the Project Plan would be replaced.

Exception Report

A description of the exception situation, its impact, options, recommendation and impact of the recommendation. This report is prepared by the Project Manager for the Project Board.

Executive

The single individual with overall responsibility for ensuring that a project meets its objectives and delivers the projected benefits. This individual should ensure that the project maintains its business focus, that it has clear authority, and that the work, including risks, is actively managed. The Executive is the chair of the Project Board. He or she represents the customer and is responsible for the Business Case.

exploit (risk response)

A risk response to an opportunity by seizing the opportunity to ensure that it will happen and that the impact will be realized.

fallback (risk response)

A risk response to a threat by putting in place a fallback plan for the actions that will be taken to reduce the impact of the threat should the risk occur.

follow-on action recommendations

Recommended actions related to unfinished work, ongoing issues and risks, and any other activities needed to take a product to the next phase of its life. These are summarized and included in the End Stage Report (for phased handover) and End Project Report.

governance (corporate)

The ongoing activity of maintaining a sound system of internal control by which the directors and officers of an organization ensure that effective management systems, including financial monitoring and control systems, have been put in place to protect assets, earning capacity and the reputation of the organization.

governance (project)

Those areas of corporate governance that are specifically related to project activities. Effective governance of project management ensures that an organization's project portfolio is aligned to the organization's objectives, is delivered efficiently and is sustainable.

handover

The transfer of ownership of a set of products to the respective user(s). The set of products is known as a release. There may be more than one handover in the life of a project (phased delivery). The final handover takes place in the Closing a Project process.

Highlight Report

A time-driven report from the Project Manager to the Project Board on stage progress.

host site

A site where project work is being undertaken (for example, an office or construction site).

impact (of risk)

The result of a particular threat or opportunity actually occurring, or the anticipation of such a result.

inherent risk

The exposure arising from a specific risk before any action has been taken to manage it.

initiation stage

The period from when the Project Board authorizes initiation to when they authorize the project (or decide not to go ahead with the project). The detailed planning and establishment of the project management infrastructure is covered by the Initiating a Project process.

issue

A relevant event that has happened, was not planned, and requires management action. It can be any concern, query, request for change, suggestion or off-specification raised during a project. Project issues can be about anything to do with the project.

Issue Register

A register used to capture and maintain information on all of the issues that are being managed formally. The Issue Register should be monitored by the Project Manager on a regular basis.

Issue Report

A report containing the description, impact assessment and recommendations for a request for change, off-specification or a problem/concern. It is only created for those issues that need to be handled formally.

Lessons Log

An informal repository for lessons that apply to this project or future projects.

Lessons Report

A report that documents any lessons that can be usefully applied to other projects. The purpose of the report is to provoke action so that the positive lessons from a project become embedded in the organization's way of working and that the organization is able to avoid the negative lessons on future projects.

logs

Informal repositories managed by the Project Manager that do not require any agreement by the Project Board on their format and composition. PRINCE2 has two logs: the Daily Log and the Lessons Log.

management product

A product that will be required as part of managing the project, and establishing and maintaining quality (for example, Highlight Report, End Stage Report etc.). The management products stay constant, whatever the type of project, and can be used as described, or with any relevant modifications, for all projects. There are three types of management product: baselines, records and reports.

management stage

The section of a project that the Project Manager is managing on behalf of the Project Board at any one time, at the end of which the Project Board will wish to review progress to date, the state of the Project Plan, the Business Case and risks, and the next Stage Plan in order to decide whether to continue with the project.

milestone

A significant event in a plan's schedule, such as completion of key Work Packages, a technical stage, or a management stage.

off-specification

Something that should be provided by the project, but currently is not (or is forecast not to be) provided. This might be a missing product or a product not meeting its specifications. It is one type of issue.

operational and maintenance acceptance

A specific type of acceptance by the person or group who will support the product once it is handed over into the operational environment.

outcome

The result of change, normally affecting real-world behaviour and/or circumstances. Outcomes are desired when a change is conceived. They are achieved as a result of the activities undertaken to effect the change.

output

A specialist product that is handed over to a user(s). Note that management products are not outputs but are created solely for the purpose of managing the project.

performance targets

A plan's goals for time, cost, quality, scope, benefits and risk.

plan

A detailed proposal for doing or achieving something which specifies the what, when, how and by whom. In PRINCE2 there are only the following types of plan: Project Plan, Stage Plan, Team Plan, Exception Plan and Benefits Review Plan.

planned closure

The PRINCE2 activity to close a project.

planning horizon

The period of time for which it is possible to accurately plan.

portfolio

All the programmes and stand-alone projects being undertaken by an organization, a group of organizations, or an organizational unit.

premature closure

The PRINCE2 activity to close a project before its planned closure. The Project Manager must ensure that work in progress is not simply abandoned, but that the project salvages any value created to date, and checks that any gaps left by the cancellation of the project are raised to corporate or programme management.

prerequisites (plan)

Any fundamental aspects that must be in place, and remain in place, for a plan to succeed.

PRINCE2

A method that supports some selected aspects of project management. The acronym stands for Projects in a Controlled Environment.

PRINCE2 principles

The guiding obligations for good project management practice that form the basis of a project being managed using PRINCE2.

PRINCE2 project

A project that applies the PRINCE2 principles.

probability

This is the evaluated likelihood of a particular threat or opportunity actually happening, including a consideration of the frequency with which this may arise.

problem/concern

A type of issue (other than a request for change or off-specification) that the Project Manager needs to resolve or escalate.

procedure

A series of actions for a particular aspect of project management established specifically for the project – for example, a risk management procedure.

process

A structured set of activities designed to accomplish a specific objective. A process takes one or more defined inputs and turns them into defined outputs.

producer

The person or group responsible for developing a product.

product

An input or output, whether tangible or intangible, that can be described in advance, created and tested. PRINCE2 has two types of products – management products and specialist products.

product breakdown structure

A hierarchy of all the products to be produced during a plan.

product checklist

A list of the major products of a plan, plus key dates in their delivery.

Product Description

A description of a product's purpose, composition, derivation and quality criteria. It is produced at planning time, as soon as possible after the need for the product is identified.

product flow diagram

A diagram showing the sequence of production and interdependencies of the products listed in a product breakdown structure.

Product Status Account

A report on the status of products. The required products can be specified by identifier or the part of the project in which they were developed.

product-based planning

A technique leading to a comprehensive plan based on the creation and delivery of required outputs. The technique considers prerequisite products, quality requirements and the dependencies between products.

programme

A temporary flexible organization structure created to coordinate, direct and oversee the implementation of a set of related projects and activities in order to deliver outcomes and benefits related to the organization's strategic objectives. A programme is likely to have a life that spans several years.

project

A temporary organization that is created for the purpose of delivering one or more business products according to an agreed Business Case.

project approach

A description of the way in which the work of the project is to be approached. For example, are we building a product from scratch or buying in a product that already exists?

Project Assurance

The Project Board's responsibilities to assure itself that the project is being conducted correctly. The Project Board members each have a specific area of focus for Project Assurance, namely business assurance for the Executive, user assurance for the Senior User(s), and supplier assurance for the Senior Supplier(s).

project authorization notification

Advice from the Project Board to inform all stakeholders and the host sites that the project has been authorized and to request any necessary logistical support (e.g. communication facilities, equipment and any Project Support) sufficient for the duration of the project.

Project Brief

Statement that describes the purpose, cost, time and performance requirements, and constraints for a project. It is created pre-project during the Starting up a Project process and is used during the Initiating a Project process to create the Project Initiation Documentation and its components. It is superseded by the Project Initiation Documentation and not maintained.

Project Initiation Documentation

A logical set of documents that brings together the key information needed to start the project on a sound basis and that conveys the information to all concerned with the project.

project initiation notification

Advice from the Project Board to inform all stakeholders and the host sites that the project is being initiated and to request any necessary logistical support (e.g. communication facilities, equipment and any Project Support) sufficient for the initiation stage.

project lifecycle

The period from the start-up of a project to the acceptance of the project product.

project management

The planning, delegating, monitoring and control of all aspects of the project, and the motivation of those involved, to achieve the project objectives within the expected performance targets for time, cost, quality, scope, benefits and risks.

project management team

The entire management structure of the Project Board, and Project Manager, plus any Team Manager, Project Assurance and Project Support roles.

project management team structure

An organization chart showing the people assigned to the project management team roles to be used, and their delegation and reporting relationships.

Project Manager

The person given the authority and responsibility to manage the project on a day-to-day basis to deliver the required products within the constraints agreed with the Project Board.

project mandate

An external product generated by the authority commissioning the project that forms the trigger for Starting up a Project.

project office

A temporary office set up to support the delivery of a specific change initiative being delivered as a project. If used, the project office undertakes the responsibility of the Project Support role.

Project Plan

A high-level plan showing the major products of the project, when they will be delivered and at what cost. An initial Project Plan is presented as part of the Project Initiation Documentation. This is revised as information on actual progress appears. It is a major control document for the Project Board to measure actual progress against expectations.

project product

What the project must deliver in order to gain acceptance.

Project Product Description

A special type of Product Description used to gain agreement from the user on the project's scope and requirements, to define the customer's quality expectations, and to define the acceptance criteria for the project.

Project Support

An administrative role in the project management team. Project Support can be in the form of advice and help with project management tools, guidance, administrative services such as filing, and the collection of actual data.

proximity (of risk)

The time factor of risk, i.e. when the risk may occur. The impact of a risk may vary in severity depending on when the risk occurs.

quality

The totality of features and inherent or assigned characteristics of a product, person, process, service and/or system that bears on its ability to show that it meets expectations or satisfies stated needs, requirements or specifications.

quality assurance

An independent check that products will be fit for purpose or meet requirements.

quality control

The process of monitoring specific project results to determine whether they comply with relevant standards and of identifying ways to eliminate causes of unsatisfactory performance.

quality criteria

A description of the quality specification that the product must meet, and the quality measurements that will be applied by those inspecting the finished product.

quality inspection

A systematic, structured assessment of a product carried out by two or more carefully selected people (the review team) in a planned, documented and organized fashion.

quality management

The coordinated activities to direct and control an organization with regard to quality.

Quality Management Strategy

A strategy defining the quality techniques and standards to be applied, and the various responsibilities for achieving the required quality levels, during a project.

quality management system

The complete set of quality standards, procedures and responsibilities for a site or organization. In the project context, 'sites' and 'organizations' should be interpreted as the permanent or semi-permanent organization(s) sponsoring the project work, i.e. they are 'external' to the project's temporary organization. A programme, for instance, can be regarded as a semi-permanent organization that sponsors projects – and it may have a documented quality management system.

quality records

Evidence kept to demonstrate that the required quality assurance and quality control activities have been carried out.

Quality Register

A register containing summary details of all planned and completed quality activities. The Quality Register is used by the Project Manager and Project Assurance as part of reviewing progress.

quality review

See 'quality inspection'.

quality review technique

A quality inspection technique with defined roles and a specific structure. It is designed to assess whether a product that takes the form of a document (or similar, e.g. a presentation) is complete, adheres to standards and meets the quality criteria agreed for it in the relevant Product Description. The participants are drawn from those with the necessary competence to evaluate its fitness for purpose.

quality tolerance

The tolerance identified for a product for a quality criterion defining an acceptable range of values. Quality tolerance is documented in the Project Product Description (for the project-level quality tolerance) and in the Product Description for each product to be delivered.

records

Dynamic management products that maintain information regarding project progress.

reduce (risk response)

A response to a risk where proactive actions are taken to reduce the probability of the event occurring by performing some form of control, and/or to reduce the impact of the event should it occur.

registers

Formal repositories managed by the Project Manager that require agreement by the Project Board on their format, composition and use. PRINCE2 has three registers: Issue Register, Risk Register and Quality Register.

reject (risk response)

A response to a risk (opportunity) where a conscious and deliberate decision is taken not to exploit or enhance an opportunity, having discerned that it is more economical to do so than to attempt a risk response action. The opportunity should continue to be monitored.

release

The set of products in a handover. The contents of a release are managed, tested and deployed as a single entity. See also 'handover'.

reports

Management products providing a snapshot of the status of certain aspects of the project.

request for change

A proposal for a change to a baseline. It is a type of issue.

residual risk

The risk remaining after the risk response has been applied.

responsible authority

The person or group commissioning the project (typically corporate or programme management) who has the authority to commit resources and funds on behalf of the commissioning organization.

reviewer

A person or group independent of the producer who assesses whether a product meets its requirements as defined in its Product Description.

risk

An uncertain event or set of events that, should it occur, will have an effect on the achievement of objectives. A risk is measured by a combination of the probability of a perceived threat or opportunity occurring, and the magnitude of its impact on objectives.

risk actionee

A nominated owner of an action to address a risk. Some actions may not be within the remit of the risk owner to control explicitly; in that situation there should be a nominated owner of the action to address the risk. He or she will need to keep the risk owner apprised of the situation.

risk appetite

An organization's unique attitude towards risk taking that in turn dictates the amount of risk that it considers is acceptable.

risk estimation

The estimation of probability and impact of an individual risk, taking into account predetermined standards, target risk levels, interdependencies and other relevant factors.

risk evaluation

The process of understanding the net effect of the identified threats and opportunities on an activity when aggregated together.

risk management

The systematic application of principles, approaches and processes to the tasks of identifying and assessing risks, and then planning and implementing risk responses.

Risk Management Strategy

A strategy describing the goals of applying risk management, as well as the procedure that will be adopted, roles and responsibilities, risk tolerances, the timing of risk management interventions, the tools and techniques that will be used, and the reporting requirements.

risk owner

A named individual who is responsible for the management, monitoring and control of all aspects of a particular risk assigned to them, including the implementation of the selected responses to address the threats or to maximize the opportunities.

risk profile

A description of the types of risk that are faced by an organization and its exposure to those risks.

Risk Register

A record of identified risks relating to an initiative, including their status and history.

risk response

Actions that may be taken to bring a situation to a level where exposure to risk is acceptable to the organization. These responses fall into a number of risk response categories.

risk response category

A category of risk response. For threats, the individual risk response category can be avoid, reduce, transfer, accept or share. For opportunities, the individual risk response category can be exploit, enhance, reject or share.

risk tolerance

The threshold levels of risk exposure which, when exceeded, will trigger an Exception Report to bring the situation to the attention of the Project Board. Risk tolerances could include limits on the plan's aggregated risks (e.g. cost of aggregated threats to remain less than 10% of the plan's budget), or limits on any individual threat (e.g. any threat to operational service). Risk tolerance is documented in the Risk Management Strategy.

risk tolerance line

A line drawn on the summary risk profile. Risks that appear above this line cannot be accepted (lived with) without referring them to a higher authority. For a project, the Project Manager would refer these risks to the Project Board.

role description

A description of the set of responsibilities specific to a role.

schedule

Graphical representation of a plan (for example, a Gantt chart), typically describing a sequence of tasks, together with resource allocations, which collectively deliver the plan. In PRINCE2, project activities should only be documented in the schedules associated with a Project Plan, Stage Plan or Team Plan. Actions that are allocated from day-to-day management may be documented in the relevant project log (i.e. Risk Register, Daily Log, Issue Register, Quality Register) if they do not require significant activity.

scope

For a plan, the sum total of its products and the extent of their requirements. It is described by the product breakdown structure for the plan and associated Product Descriptions.

scope tolerance

The permissible deviation in a plan's scope that is allowed before the deviation needs to be escalated to the next level of management. Scope tolerance is documented in the respective plan in the form of a note or reference to the product breakdown structure for that plan. See 'tolerance'.

Senior Responsible Owner

A UK government term for the individual responsible for ensuring that a project or programme of change meets its objectives and delivers the projected benefits. The person should be the owner of the overall business change that is being supported by the project. The Senior Responsible Owner (SRO) should ensure that the change maintains its business focus, that it has clear authority, and that the context, including risks, is actively managed. This individual must be senior and must take personal responsibility for successful delivery of the project. The SRO should be recognized as the owner throughout the organization.

The SRO appoints the project's Executive (or in some cases may elect to be the Executive).

Senior Supplier

The Project Board role that provides knowledge and experience of the main discipline(s) involved in the production of the project's deliverable(s). The Senior Supplier represents the supplier interests within the project and provides supplier resources.

Senior User

The Project Board role accountable for ensuring that user needs are specified correctly and that the solution meets those needs.

share (risk response)

A risk response to either a threat or an opportunity through the application of a pain/gain formula: both parties share the gain (within pre-agreed limits) if the cost is less than the cost plan; and both share the pain (again within pre-agreed limits) if the cost plan is exceeded.

specialist product

A product whose development is the subject of the plan. The specialist products are specific to an individual project (for example, an advertising campaign, a car park ticketing system, foundations for a building, a new business process etc.) Also known as a deliverable or output.

sponsor

The main driving force behind a programme or project. PRINCE2 does not define a role for the sponsor, but the sponsor is most likely to be the Executive on the Project Board, or the person who has appointed the Executive.

stage

See 'management stage' or 'technical stage'.

Stage Plan

A detailed plan used as the basis for project management control throughout a stage.

stakeholder

Any individual, group or organization that can affect, be affected by, or perceive itself to be affected by, an initiative (programme, project, activity, risk).

start-up

The pre-project activities undertaken by the Executive and the Project Manager to produce the outline Business Case, Project Brief and Initiation Stage Plan.

strategy

An approach or line to take, designed to achieve a long-term aim. Strategies can exist at different levels – at the corporate, programme and project level. At the project level, PRINCE2 defines four strategies: Communication Management Strategy, Configuration Management Strategy, Quality Management Strategy and Risk Management Strategy.

supplier

The person, group or groups responsible for the supply of the project's specialist products.

tailoring

The appropriate use of PRINCE2 on any given project, ensuring that there is the correct amount of planning, control, governance and use of the processes and themes (whereas the adoption of PRINCE2 across an organization is known as 'embedding').

Team Manager

The person responsible for the production of those products allocated by the Project Manager (as defined in a Work Package) to an appropriate quality, timescale and at a cost acceptable to the Project Board. This role reports to, and takes direction from, the Project Manager. If a Team Manager is not assigned, then the Project Manager undertakes the responsibilities of the Team Manager role.

Team Plan

An optional level of plan used as the basis for team management control when executing Work Packages.

technical stage

A method of grouping work together by the set of techniques used, or the products created. This results in stages covering elements such as design, build and implementation. Such stages are technical stages and are a separate concept from management stages.

theme

An aspect of project management that needs to be continually addressed, and that requires specific treatment for the PRINCE2 processes to be effective.

time tolerance

The permissible deviation in a plan's time that is allowed before the deviation needs to be escalated to the next level of management. Time tolerance is documented in the respective plan. See also 'tolerance'.

time-driven control

A management control that is periodic in nature, to enable the next higher authority to monitor progress – e.g. a control that takes place every two weeks. PRINCE2 offers two key time-driven progress reports: Checkpoint Report and Highlight Report.

tolerance

The permissible deviation above and below a plan's target for time and cost without escalating the deviation to the next level of management. There may also be tolerance levels for quality, scope, benefit and risk. Tolerance is applied at project, stage and team levels.

tranche

A programme management term describing a group of projects structured around distinct step changes in capability and benefit delivery.

transfer (risk response)

A response to a threat where a third party takes on responsibility for some of the financial impact of the threat (for example, through insurance or by means of appropriate clauses in a contract).

trigger

An event or decision that triggers a PRINCE2 process.

user

The person or group who will use one or more of the project's products.

user acceptance

A specific type of acceptance by the person or group who will use the product once it is handed over into the operational environment.

variant

A variation on a baselined product. For example, an operations manual may have an English variant and a Spanish variant.

version

A specific baseline of a product. Versions typically use naming conventions that enable the sequence or date of the baseline to be identified. For example, Project Plan version 2 is the baseline after Project Plan version 1.

waterfall method

A development approach that is linear and sequential with distinct goals for each phase of development. Once a phase of development is completed, the development proceeds to the next phase and earlier phases are not revisited (hence the analogy that water flowing down a mountain cannot go back).

Work Package

The set of information relevant to the creation of one or more products. It will contain a description of the work, the Product Description(s), details of any constraints on production, and confirmation of the agreement between the Project Manager and the person or Team Manager who is to implement the Work Package that the work can be done within the constraints.

Index

Index